Smalley

West Virginia Logging Railroads

by

William E. Warden

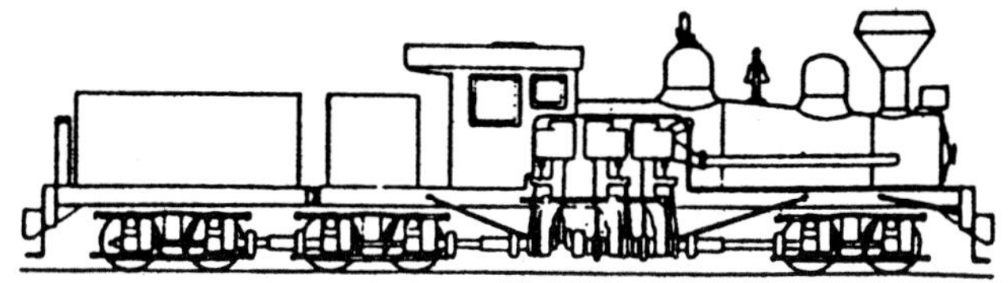

TLC
PUBLISHING INC.

1997
TLC Publishing Inc.
1387 Winding Creek Lane
Lynchburg, Virginia • 24503-3776

Front Cover Illustration: *This original painting by Richard M. Sparks, noted West Virginia logging historian and painter, depicts Elk River Coal & Lumber Company Shay No. 19 fording the Lilly Fork. Elk River Coal and Lumber''s logging railroad was known for its lack of bridges and its frequent fords. After all, logging lines changed constantly as different parts of the forest were worked, so there was no need to install substantial bridges any more than there was any need for a ballasted or tie-plated roadway.*

This book is dedicated to the memory of

John Krause

June 16, 1929 - April 30, 1989

who believed in me enough to publish my first railroad book, and whose photography liberally graces this book.

Johnny Krause, with his booming "Noo Yawk"-accented voice and 4x5 press camera, was a familiar figure to those of us who practiced our train watching avocation in the hills and forests of The Mountain State. But Johnny had the courage to venture forth in search of the perfect photograph where few of the faithful went. In the process, he, probably more than anyone, defined West Virginia logging railroad photography as an art form. We can only hope that, in death, Johnny has been rewarded with a never-ending parade of Shays, Climaxes, and Heislers pounding up some celestial grade. God be with you, John.

— Bill Warden

FIRST PRINTING, 1994
SECOND PRINTING, 1995
THIRD PRINTING, 1996
FOURTH PRINTING, 1998
FIFTH PRINTING, 1999

Library of Congress Catalog Number 93-60885
ISBN 1-883089-03-4

Typography and Layout
by
Tom & Carolyn Dixon

Printed by
Walsworth Publishing Co.
Marceline, Missouri 64658

Contents

Acknowledgements

We can only acknowledge with considerable humility the contributions made by many dedicated and loyal friends and colleagues to the writing of this book. Any credit for the quality and readability of this work must go to them more than to me.

Those to whom I owe an eternal debt of gratitude include: Roy Clarkson, who was kind enough to share his knowledge of West Virginia logging lore with me; Phil Bagdon and George Deike, whose comments, suggestions, and criticism helped clear up much of the confusion about the subject; Dave Marquis who provided some valuable insights into Elk River Coal & Lumber rail operations; Bill Reddy who went the extra mile to find information about Ely-Thomas Lumber; Kenny Funderburke and Rod Neal, who opened a gold mine of Ely-Thomas anecdotes; the late Benjamin F. G. Kline who supplied vintage logging photographs from the Pennsylvania State Railroad Museum; Bill Nelson for being a treasure trove of Cherry River Boom & Lumber information; Richard Sparks for clearing up the mystery of the type of valve gear used on geared locomotives; Ed Crist, who allowed me the pick of his John Krause and Phil Ronfor photo collection; Lloyd D. Lewis who supplied several John Krause photos from his negative collection and did editorial work; Harold Vollrath whose historic photos are a welcome addition to any railroad book; photographers Charles Winters, Richard J. Cook, Sr., and Howard Ameling who filled in some important gaps in the book's illustrations; August Thieme who took the trouble to furnish much of the Ely-Thomas logging information and photos unavailable elsewhere; Bill McNeel, editor of *The Pocahontas Times,* who supplied photos much historical information from his newspaper's files on logging in the Greenbrier Valley; Jim Comstock, editor of *The West Virginia Hillbilly* , who was kind enough to publish my plea for logging railroad information in his newspaper; Jim Gwinn, who supplied much information to Meadow River Lumber's history; Russ Hass who drew the maps that help the reader visualize the geography of each railroad; and a special thank you is due to Tom Lawson, whose patience in preparing and correcting locomotive roster information and in coping with my general ignorance, would have made Job seem like a positive hot-head.

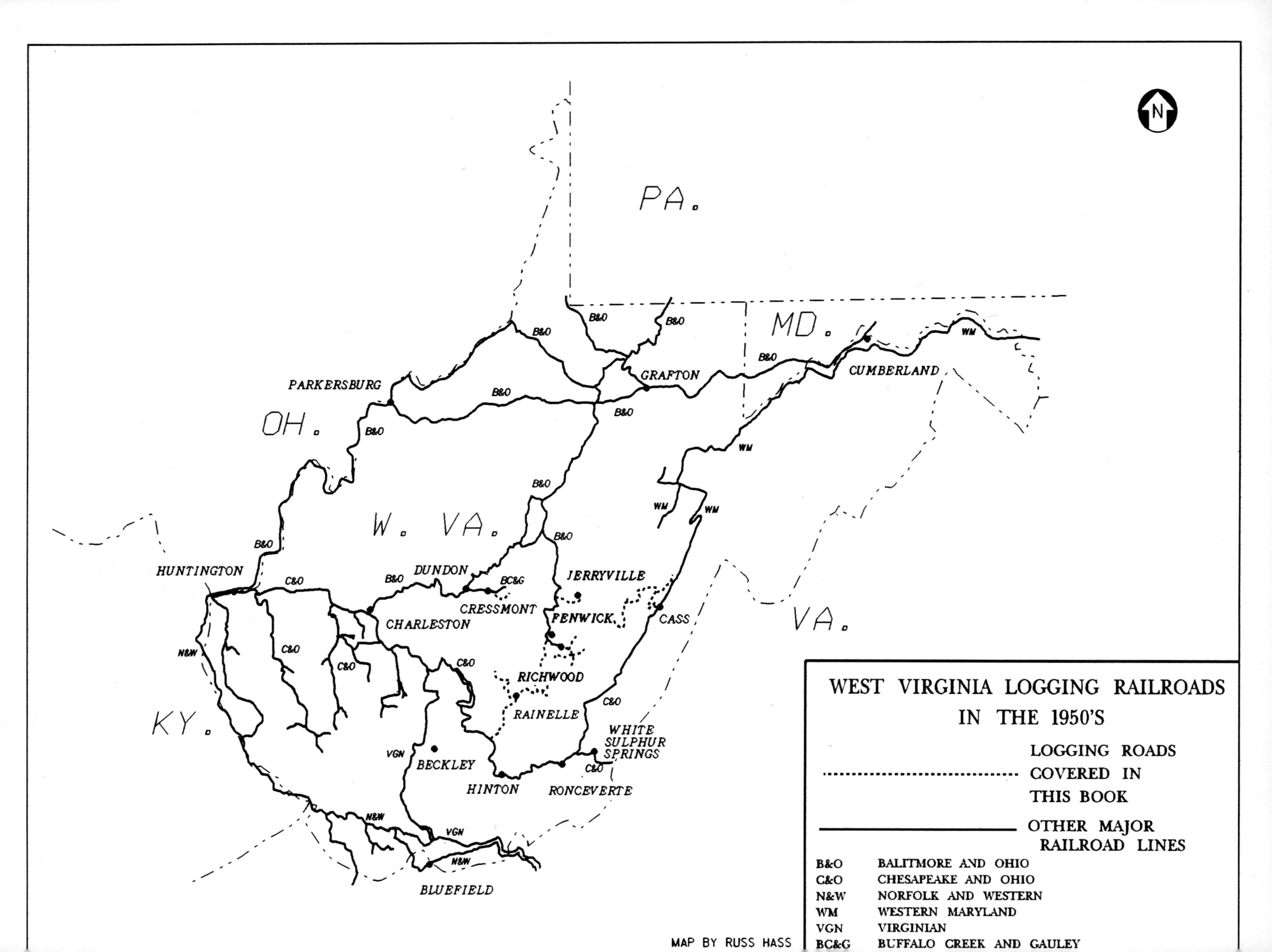

MAP BY RUSS HASS

Introduction

This is the story about a strange, beautiful, harsh land, always in conflict with itself, and about one of its more important modes of transportation.

This is a story about a land of paradoxes and contradictions; a land that gave welcome to all and quarter to none; a land where vistas of natural grandeur, unrivaled on the planet, sat cheek-by-jowl with four generations of grinding poverty; a land that would give birth to the gentle writer Pearl Buck and where a man like the aptly-named "Devil Anse" Hatfield of feuding a fame could flourish; a land where men would shower the stranger with kindness and generosity while going out of their way to avoid the neighbor because of some slight, real or fancied, that had occurred 30 years ago; a land where John L. Lewis, Samuel Gompers, and Mother Jones did battle with guns, guile, and bombs to spread the gospel of unionism, and simple country preachers did battle with words and example to spread the Gospel of love and forgiveness.

This then is abook about West Virginia and its logging railroads.

Picture the scene.....

You, the trusting and unsuspecting train watcher, have suddenly been plopped down amid this jumble of green hills and narrow valleys, seemingly strewn about at random by The Creator. Pure West Virginia.

While you are trying to get your bearings and figure out which way is north, you hear the unmistakable wail of a steam locomotive whistle in the distance. But where's the track? A few moments' searching uncovers two spindly rails spiked to untreated ties placed in a rhodendron grove. Tie plates and ballasted roadbed are conspicuous by their absence.

Nothing more happens for four, maybe five, minutes. Then suddenly there emerges from around a bend a smoke plume of proportions befitting a Norfolk & Western 2-8-8-2 assaulting Blue Ridge Grade or a C&O 2-6-6-6 getting a coal drag out of Hinton. The plume moves with glacier-like rapidity in your direction. Surely this is a slow and heavy freight. But now you hear the rapid feathery exhaust typical of, say *The Pocahontas* or *The Sportsman* making fifty or sixty miles per hour.

While you are contemplating this seeming contradiction of audio and visual signals, from around the bend comes this lopsided locomotive with strange vertical cylinders all on one side, flailing rods, gears, and shafts, and drive wheels impossibly small. A brakeman takes his ease atop the engine's pilot beam. Following the engine comes a stubby tender and a dozen or so truss-rodded flat cars riding on arch bar trucks and bearing logs of impressive girth. You reckon that two very tall men would be hard pressed to lock hands around one of the logs. Finally, tied to the last flat comes this little four-wheel bobber of a wooden caboose. You have just seen a typical West Virginia logging train going flat out for the mill.

Forty or fifty years ago, with minor variations, you could have witnessed this operation two dozen or more times a day, five or six days a week, in various parts of The Mountain State. Today, you will see it nowhere, for those logging companies that haven't gone out of business have opted to transport the logs by motor truck. The purpose of this book is to look at how, where, and why these little dramas were played out by focusing on some of the many logging railroads that wound through West Virginia. These roads have been selected on the basis of their being among the biggest and last surviving ones, and hence, ones the average reader may have heard of.

We will also examine these unique locomotives so that we may understand why they were so essential to the lumbering industry. The highly technical aspects of locomotive design and operation have been covered in great detail by other authors; this examination is designed to provide a working knowledge of the intricacies of Heislers, Shays, and Climaxes for those who already have comparable knowledge of conventional rod locomotives. And because the business of operating a logging railroad was inextricably entwined with the business of running a logging operation, we will also offer a brief history of logging in West Virginia.

Then, when you have acquired a more than nodding acquaintance with West Virginia logging practices and have become an instant expert on logging locomotives, it will be time to examine some of the more significant loggers in detail. "Significant" can be interpreted in several ways; for purposes of this book, it denotes roads that in their lifetime moved large amounts of timber and also lasted into relative modern times.

One of the tenets of journalism that was hammered into this writer as a cub reporter in his misspent youth was that if you are writing a long story, you put the most important facts near the beginning and save the lesser ones for later. Applying this tenet to this book, the author has arranged the various chapters on the individual logging roads in what he considers their proper order of importance. Since this is a personal judgement, readers are free to disagree with the order. And if we left out your pet logger, we apologize but space limitations prohibit trying to cover in one book the history of the more than 100 logging railroads that ran at one time in The Mountain State.

So, settle back and enjoy the medley of the aroma of soft coal smoke mingled with that of fresh sawdust, and the cacaphony of shotgun exhausts vying with the whine of double-band mills.

All ready?

William E. Warden
Waynesboro, Virginia
January 1994

Publisher's Note: We regret to announce that Bill Warden passed away on February 10, 1994, just as this book was going to press. We are particularly saddened at the loss of this fine man and his expertise as a railroad photographer as well as his warm and folksy style of history. Bill will be missed by his family and friends, and by the railroad history community at large in which he was a giant.

This scene, far back in the mountains west of Bald Knob, combines several important elements in the logging railroad story. The giant boom of a Lidgerwood log skidder towers over the log train which has a steam operated log loader mounted atop its crude flat cars, while smoke from its Shay motive power is visible to the right. - John Killoran photo.

Chapter 1 - West Virginia Logging History Background

It is said that when the first Scotch-Irish settlers pushed across the Alleghany Mountains into what is now West Virginia, the land was so densely forested that a squirrel could travel from the crest of the Alleghanies to the Ohio River without once setting foot on ground.

A bit of hyperbole? Perhaps. But reliable observers of the late-18th and early-19th centuries report seas of oak, hickory, tulip poplar, walnut, and pine stretching to the horizon. At higher elevations, where the local climate was not unlike that of southern New England, there were sugar maples, the highly-prized spruce—an estimated 220,000 acres in Pocahontas County alone—hemlock, and birches. And everywhere was the immensely useful and practically indestructible chestnut tree. The chestnut blight reached West Virginia around the end of World War I, however, and by 1923 there was scarcely a live chestnut left in the state.

A tall man could easily walk through these forests without being brushed; first limbs 70 or 80 feet above the ground on trees 8 or 9 feet in diameter were common in the state, while overhead, the dense foliage shut off the daylight and prevented growth of most underbrush. Even as late as 1870, it was estimated that more than 60 percent of the land was still virgin forest.

The early settlers were not lumbermen, however. To them the vast forests were at best a source of lumber for their own houses and furniture; at worst, they were a nuisance that interfered with plowing and planting. When you consider that the most advanced implement a settler had for attacking a log as big in diameter as he was tall was a two-handled whipsaw, it is easy to see why timber was not considered a cash crop. Two burly sawyers could barely turn out 100 feet of cut lumber in one day with a whipsaw.

But as more people settled in western Virginia, a demand for cut and dressed lumber for houses, stores, banks, and churches sprung up. The demand was met by primitive water-powered sawmills which began to appear just before the American Revolution in what is now West Virginia. These early mills were little more than mechanized whipsaws, or "sash" saws, with a mechanized carriage to carry the logs and force them against the saw blade, but they represented a quantum leap in productivity; now two saywers could turn out about 500 linear feet of lumber per day.

Improvements continued to be made to these early mills, including the installation of "gang saws" or multiple blades that could saw out several boards simul-taneously from one log. Ultimately, a single water mill could turn out 30,000 or more linear feet of board in one day. However, it was two products of the Industrial Revolution of the early 1800s that were to turn logging into big business: the steam engine and the circular saw.

Clearly, a water mill had its limitations. To power the water wheel it was necessary to locate the mill on the fall line of a river or at least where there were rapids. And in time of droughts, when waterflow was greatly reduced, so was the mill's output of boards. In winter, when a stream was frozen over, output dropped even further.

But a steam-powered mill was unaffected by weather or stream level; mills could now be built wherever convenient, usually along fairly calm and wide parts of a stream, so that logs could be stored and cleaned of dirt in a pond (whence comes the expression "Calm as a mill pond") until ready for cutting—a practice still common within the memory of the author. And the circular saw, invented in England in 1877, was a much simpler and faster device than a sash saw. By the 1840s the steam-powered circular sawmill was firmly

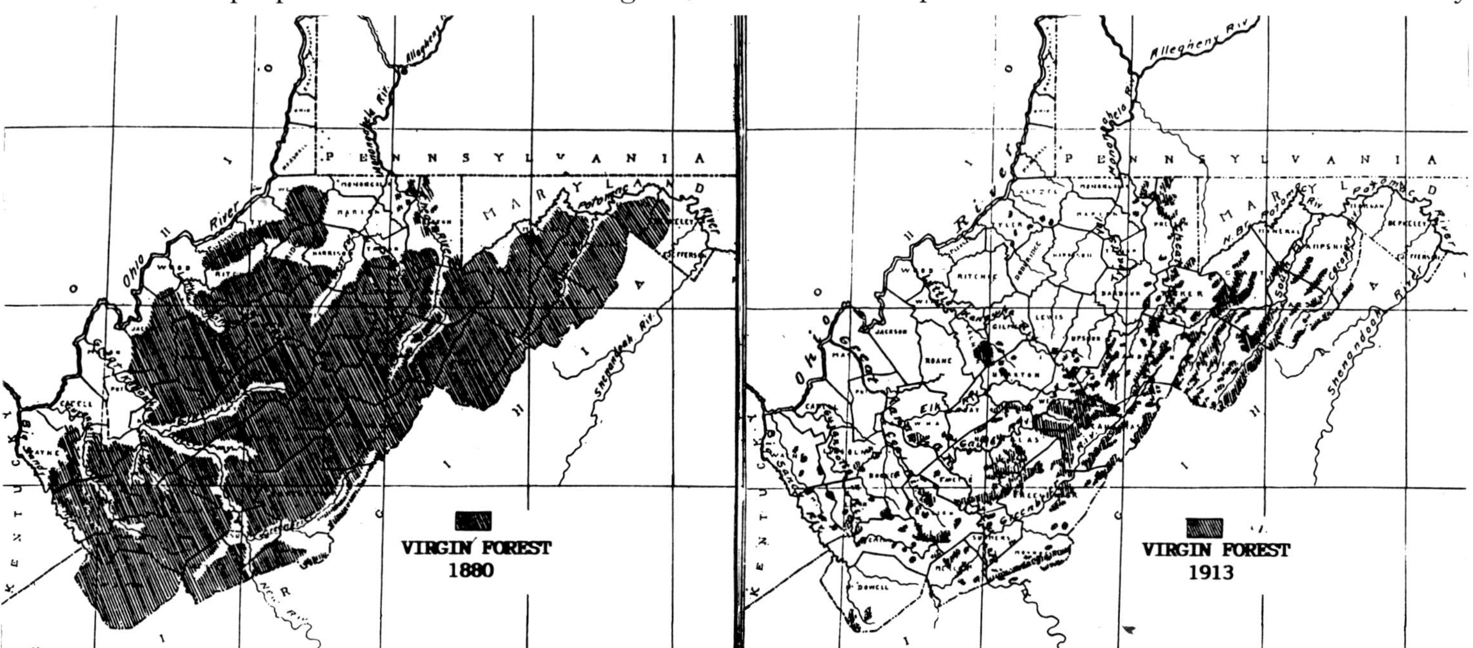

Comparison of the extent of virgin forest land in West Virginia in 1880(left) and in 1913 (right). This graphically illustrates the efficiency of late 19th Century logging operations in the state, made possible by the development of the band sawmill and the geared logging locomotive. (Maps from *A Semi-Centennial History of West Virginia* by James M. Callahan, 1913.)

established in the counties that now form West Virginia. Reputedly the largest circular sawmill (134 feet long, 60 feet wide, and 50 feet high), the St. Lawrence Boom and Manufacturing Mill at Ronceverte, could saw 120,000 feet of lumber in one day.

For all its increased efficiency, the circular saw had two shortcomings: (1) Practical considerations of keeping it rigid while keeping the "kerf" (or portion of each cut reduced to sawdust) limited to approximately 1/2 inch, restricted the diameter of a saw blade to approximately eight feet, which meant that the deepest cut possible was somewhat under four feet. Hence a large log could not be cut into individual boards with a single cut on a circular saw. (2) Logs could be cut while moving in one direction only.

Overcoming the first objection required a process sometimes known as "slabbing." A large log would be mechanically rotated 90 degrees and slabs cut off until there remained a more-or-less square piece of lumber. Then the individual slabs and the squared log were moved to an updated version of the gang mill where they were cut into boards of the required thickness and width.

Overcoming the second shortcoming required the development of a brand new technology—the band saw. First patented in France in 1834 and the U. S. in 1835, the band saw consisted of a single flexible steel band anywhere from 10 to 16 inches wide and 30 to 45 feet long running continuously over wheels having diameters ranging 5 to 11 feet. With the blade held taut by the two wheels, kerf could be limited to 1/4 inch regardless of the depth of the cut. Since both edges of the saw blade always traveled in the same direction, teeth could be put on both edges and logs cut while moving in either direction. Sawmills that used bands with teeth on both edges were known as "double-cutting band mills." The sound of a double-cutting band mill in heat was extremely loud, but then, by way of compensation, few industries perfumed the air with anything as sweet as the smell of new sawdust.

Problems with joining the two ends of the band and finding mechanics who could keep the saw teeth sharp limited the use of band mills until 1881 when the first one was built at Charleston. They never totally supplanted circular sawmills, although more than 260 operated at one time or another in the state. By the 1880s, logging had become a major West Virginia industry and the wholesale cutting down of virgin forests, both to the betterment and detriment of the state, was irrreversibly underway.

Some idea how the logging industry flourished and then waned as the timber played out can be gained from the U. S. Department of Commerce figures in the illustration on page 3, which compares the amounts of virgin forest land in 1880 and 1913, and the table below

Year	**Million Board feet of lumber***
1889	302
1899	778
1909	1,473
1919	763
1929	633
1939	324
1947	484
1949	480
1963	445

(*One board foot is equivalent to a slab one foot square by one inch thick).

As can be seen from the table, West Virginia logging peaked in 1909 and it was mostly downhill thereafter as the virgin forests were gradually cut over. The slight upturn in 1947 can be attributed to the postwar housing boom that suddenly made it economical to cut some of the remoter stands of timber that were left untouched in earlier days.

While we've been busy sawing up logs, we've neglected to get them from the forest to the mill in the first place, so let's correct that now. Until the advent of the chain saw in the late 1940s, the process of cutting down trees and cutting up logs varied little from that used in the late 19th Century. A typical logging crew consisted of six men. One, known as the "chopper" or "fitter" was responsible for notching the tree in the direction in which it was to fall. Two sawyers, armed with a six-foot cross-cut saw, would start cutting above and on the side opposite the notch. Periodically, wedges were hammered into the cut to prevent the saw from

John Krause

In this anachronistic scene, a Cherry River Boom and Lumber Co. train loads logs being skidded by horses, a practice generally discontinued when the steam skidders came into general use. The log loader is lifting a large trunk onto the flat as CRB&L 2-8-2 No. 15 waits patiently on the head end. CRB&L was one of the few West Virginia loggers to use rod locomotives.

binding. Once a tree was felled, three "knott bumpers" would trim off the smaller limbs and then "nose" each log, that is, cut a bevel on each end that would make it easier to maneuver the log around rocks, stumps, etc. In addition to their pay, these "wood hicks" were fed at company expense four squares a day, any one of which would have been sufficient to sustain their more sedentary kinsmen for a whole day.

Although all that sounds easy, hours were long and logging was strenuous physical labor, for which the men were paid $1.50 to $1.75 a day. A good sawyer, by comparison, with less than a high school education made as much as his college-bred brother holding down a prestigious desk job in the city. For the sawyer was the man who ran the saw in the mill and judged each log to get the most and best lumber out of it. In return for this compensation, the wood hick worked outdoors in rain, snow (unless it became too deep to wade through), sleet, bitter cold, and in blazing heat. To be fair about it, West Virginia winters are considerably more oppressive than its summers. And when his day's labors were over, he repaired to a logging camp whose accommodations were at best spartan and often enough to horrify a Trappist monk. (More on these logging camps and logger's life will be found in Chapter 3.) Logging was definitely not a career to be pursued by those who essayed creature comforts.

Felling the trees and sawing them into logs of manageable lengths was only half of the job; still remaining was was skidding the logs to the stream or logging railroad that would take them to the mill. Horses were the means of doing this initially. Use of wooden skids gave rise to such common slang expression as "greasing the skids," and "on the skids."

A teamster had one of the most dangerous jobs in a logging camp; if a "train" of logs headed down hill broke loose and headed off on its own, the driver's and horses' lives were in danger.

Several means of getting the logs down hill faster and with less peril to the teamster and his steeds were developed. One means was the "log slide." This was basically a trough of logs resting on round ties that kept the logs in line. One standard trough ploy was to wet down the logs on a winter night so that a sheet of ice encasing each trough log would reduce the friction the next day. Grease or petroleum performed the same function in the summer months.

Skidding had one disadvantage that was overlooked for many years: troughs built to follow the line of least resistance for logs also followed the line of least resistance for rain water. Thus, a real gully-washer eroded large quantities of topsoil around the skids. And without topsoil, reforesting the land was nearly impossible. The problem was somewhat solved in the late 1940s when Caterpiller and International Harvester tractors began replacing horses. Now skid roads could follow the natural contours of the land—indeed, it was almost greatly reduced, although by no means eliminated.

Despite improvements offered by the trough, skidding logs remained a backbreaking and dangerous job until the Lidgerwood Company of New York introduced the steam-powered Lidgerwood Skidder in the late 1890s. The first Lidgerwoods in West Virginia were installed near Davis in Tucker County in 1904. Skidders could be either mounted on the ground or placed on a flatcar that sat on rails of its own. A picture of a rail-mounted skidder can be seen on page 71.

Explaining the complex Lidgerwood is beyond the scope of this book. Suffice to say that, containing as much as a mile of 1-7/8-inch cable capable of reaching 2,600 feet to transport the lgos; it was one of the largest and most sophisticated steam-driven machines ever built. However, the horse is a durable creature and some of the loggers—Cherry River Boom & Lumber Company for one—eschewed the coal-burning Lidgerwood in some locations in favor of "oat burners" well into the 1950s.

Now that we've gotten the logs out of the woods, let's get them to the mill.

Where it was impractical to skid logs directly to the mill, early loggers constructed tram roads.

Typically, the tram consisted of hardwood planks nailed to stringers. The planks provided footing for the horses and kept the wagons they pulled from bogging down in the mud. Later, wooden rails were nailed to the planks and the wagons were equipped with flanged iron wheels to reduce friction. Tram roads became common in the late 1880s.

Tram roads were practical as long as the loggers remained within a few miles of the mill. But as logging operations bored deeper into the West Virginia mountains, or if there was no relatively level space in which to build one, the tram road became impractical. Additionally, every wagon required at minimum a driver and, more often than not, a brakeman as well as a team of horses.

But there was the river or stream ready to carry logs directly to the mill, and water power to get them there was free. Manpower was not free, however, and the process of getting logs to the mill courtesy of a convenient stream was, as we shall see, quite labor intensive.

If a stream was deep enough, log rafts were the method of choice. (Rafting also was used to transport finished lumber from mills to railroads at one time.) Seventy or so logs would be lashed to poles at right angles to them by means of "chain dogs" consisting of two wedges joined by a chain. Chain dogs made disassembling a raft at the mill easy and of course they could be used again repeatedly, but in some cases, the logs were simply nailed to the cross poles.

Now, you don't just set a log raft adrift and expect the raft to arrive at the mill intact. If you have ever traveled through the New River Gorge aboard Amtrak's *Cardinal*, particularly at times of low water, you have seen just how full of rocks and other pesky objects to break up or snag a raft a mountain stream can be. Hence a pilot was needed to steer each raft around obstacles. Huge oars on the ends of a raft were used to change the raft's course. The pilot was the "brain surgeon of lumbering" and was paid accordingly. He had to anticipate every obstacle; if he misjudged the exact

Westvaco , W. P. McNeel Coll.

Two lumberjacks in traditional pose jockey an errant log back into the log drive in this early scene on the Greenbrier River. Quite a balancing act on a log that might roll over and dump its handlers at any moment!

location of an underwater rock, its whole crew of men who traveled on board spent considerable time dislodging the raft, or worse yet, the raft was destroyed and the men hurt or drowned.

Where a stream was too shallow or fast-running to accomodate a raft, log drives were employed. Log drives on the Greenbrier River flourished from the mid 1870s until 1908.

The image of the agile lumberjack jumping from log to log in the swirling stream to break a log jam is a standard fixture of folklore. In this author's opinion, the most realistic and gritty description of a log drive on the Greenbrier River to Ronceverte is contained in Warren Blackhurst's fictional *Riders of the Flood* and I recommend you read it. Breaking up a log jam in icy water where one slip meant death in a particularly unpleasant manner was not glamorous at all.

Drives usually began about the time ice broke up in a stream in March or April. Old-timers recall ice as thick as 12 inches on the Greenbrier and when it began breaking up, you could hear the roar a mile away. Because a large crew of men following a drive was necessary to free logs from a jam, a floating bunkhouse known as an "ark" provided sleeping quarters for a logging crew on the week or longer trip. A second ark held a kitchen and dining room in which the men all took their meals.

Once a drive reached the mill, a large "boom" (a dam of connected logs) across the stream corralled the timber into the holding pond. A heavy chain with cleats known as a "bull chain" was used to carry logs to the mill.

Movies, fiction, and country log rolling contests have unfairly romanticized the lumberjack's lives. A good man might make as much as a plant superintendent in a week, but what is romantic about working a 10- or 12-hour day constantly soaked by cold water, with your own life and those of your buddies always in danger?

Westvaco Photo, W. P. McNeel Coll.

One of the log drive "arks" being loaded with provisions on the Greenbrier River at Marlinton. Note the covered bridge in the background.

Paul J. Dolkas

Shay No. 19 simmers, as W. M. Ritter Lumber Co. log loader rides rails laid on one flatcar while loading another a typical scene late in the logging era, in August 1959.

As logging companies had to venture further afield to find trees suitable for cutting, the costs of skidding logs to a stream and then floating them to the mill increased accordingly. Now, if there were just a safe and economical way to transport logs from where they were cut directly to the mill without resorting to slides, or rafts, or drives....The answer was the logging railroad and the steam-operated log loader.

This latter device, similar in appearance to a railroad wrecking crane or "big hook," but with tongs instead of a hook, came in several versions. The most popular types in West Virginia, the American and Barnhart log loaders, were able to winch themselves back and forth on rails laid atop flatcars. A short section of track was carried along to bridge the gaps between cars and allow the loader to move from car to car. Brake wheel shafts on the flats were pivoted so they could be swung out of the way of loaders crossing from car to car. To compensate for the uneveness of these portable tracks, log loader wheels usually had flanges both on the inside (like regular rail car wheels) and on the outside. In some cases, dual-gauge wheels—that is pairs of wheels sharing a common flange—were used.

A less common version, the McGiffert swinging boom log loader, rode directly on the railroad rails but had provisions for showing logging flats under it—or to be be more technical, through it—on a portable "shoofly" track. Either type could be hauled by a logging train to the site where the logs had been skidded.

American also made a loader, the Model "D," that road directly on the logging track instead of atop flat cars, but which did not require a "shoofly." In addition it was self-propelled. Because of its low center of gravity and the fact that it had stabilizing beams extended out from the frame that could be wedged up on the tie ends, the "D" was favored by narrow gauge loggers. Pardee & Curtin Lumber Co. had at least three narrow gauge "Ds."

Normal operating procedure with a "D" consisted of the loader picking up an empty skeleton flat car, setting it on the track in front of the loader, loading it and pushing it out of the way, then repeating the process until an entire train had been loaded. Since a skeleton flat—which was little more than a couple of wooden beams mounted on arch-bar tricks—weighed on the order of four tons, muscling it around this was was well within the loader's capabilities. A photo of an Ely-Thomas Class "D" loader is shown on this page.

In the next several chapters we'll get acquainted with the locomotives that made logging railroads possible and see how those unusual railroads and the men who ran them went about their jobs of taming the West Virginia forests.

August A. Thieme

(Left) An Ely-Thomas Lumber Co. American type log loader moves a skeleton flat car, none too gently, into position for loading at a logging camp somewhere up Laurel Creek in Greenbrier County, October 1954. Although most log loaders rode atop the flat cars that they loaded, some, like this one road directly on the logging road's track and moved empty cars from behind it to the front so they could be loaded one at a time.

John Krause

(Right) Meadow River Lumber Co. loader lofts oversized logs onto a flat and idler while crew of Heisler No. 6 inspect some malfunction. Tracks of the C&O/NYC jointly owned Nicholas, Fayette & Greenbrier Railroad (over which Meadow River trains operated to get to the woods) are in the background. Meadow River's practice was to wait until the logs got to the mill to cut them into manageable lengths.

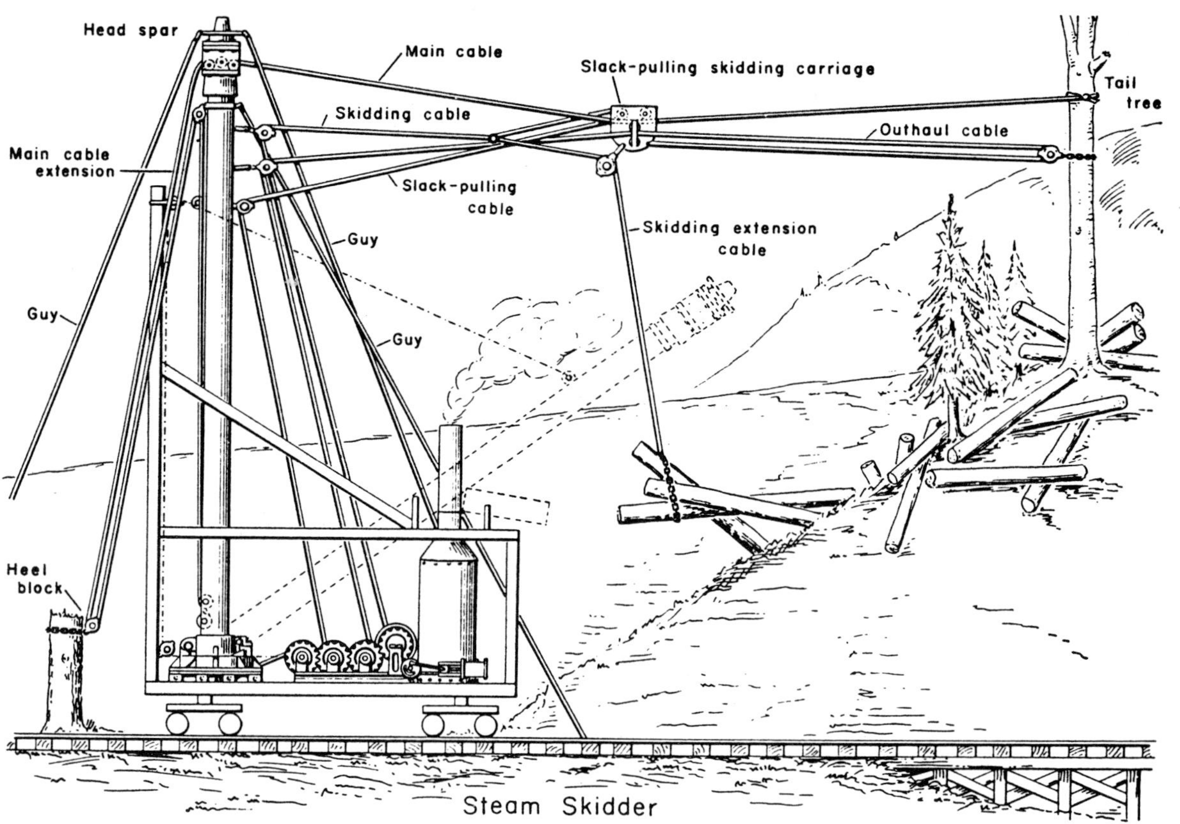

From *Tumult on The Mountains*, by Roy B. Clarkson McClain Printing Co., Parsons, W. Va.

(Above) The Lidgerwood skidder was a very effective though complicated steam-operated machine. A cable was affixed to a distant tree and a series of other cables and pulleys were used to pull logs toward the skidder where they could be loaded on the log train. ***(Below, left)*** A Mower Lumber Co. crew and skidder about 26 miles up the mountain from Cass, West Virginia, await arrival of a log train powered by Shay No. 1.—Note the complicated series of cables connecting to the tower. ***(Below, right)*** Repairing the head spar of a Mower Lidgerwood skidder in November 1956. The view must have been great but the work, like much of logging, dangerous.

(both) Phil Ronfor, Ed Crest Coll.

Ely-Thomas's stubby narrow-gauge logging flats give new meaning to the term "primitive." But when nobody but your own employees and a few dedicated train watchers are going to see it, what's wrong with slapping something like this together in your own shop? Air brakes?—Don't be ridiculous! This photo was taken at Saxman in July 1956.

(both) Phil Ronfor, Ed Crist Coll.

Careful there! The man at right is using a pike pole to guide logs on the jack slip, or gangway, the inclined plane used for moving logs from the mill pond into the mill. The pond is property of Elk River Coal & Lumber Co., and is located at Swandale.

Richard J. Cook, Sr.

The two loads of logs that Shay No. 12 just brought into Swandale are being unloaded into the mill pond beside the Elk River Coal & Lumber Co. Mill in August 1953. They will float in the pond until needed, then will be conveyed into the big band saw mill by means of the jack slip. Note the men with pikes guiding the logs in as shown in detail in the middle photo.

Chapter 2 - The Loggers' Iron Horses

If you were designing a West Virginia logging railroad and its motive power, what specifications would you draw up? Remember, speed is unimportant because *anything* you design will be faster than tram roads or log rafts.

Well, for starters, since the road must go to where the loggers are and that is going to change as different parts of the forest are cut, the track must be portable. Forget about grading a roadbed and other niceties; your roadbed is to be bare earth. Use a track gauge? Well, maybe. Treated ties? Don't be silly; your track crews will skin some short logs, throw them down on the roadbed and spike some rails to them; the track'll be moved long before the ties rot. Just as long as the rails can be moved quickly to another location, no one will care. A typical haphazard track laying operation is illustrated on this page.

This pretty much limited the rail weight to about 75 pounds per yard, and if you can squeeze by with 50-pound rail, so much the better. Then too, rail that's spiked to uneven logs and that gets moved frequently even by experienced track crews is going to develop kinks and bumps, so whatever rides these rails must be impervious to unevenness.

Next, if you must get track right up in the mountain to where the cutting is going on, you must consider sharp curves—as sharp as 35 degrees, and steep grades—at least 6 percent, even with switchbacks. Your motive power is going to need good traction and braking capabilities, particularly if you don't plan on using air brakes on your logging flat cars.

Figure on maximum loads on your ruling grades of, say, 150 or 200 tons. If you can pull 1,000 or 1,300 tons on grades less than 1 percent, so much the better. Remember, speed's not important; starting tractive effort is, however.

Having assembled all these parameters, you can now decide what features your motive power should have. If we're to maintain adhesion on those stiff grades, we'll need lots of drive wheels—at least 8, and 12 or 16 would be better. An if we're going to maximize tractive effort at low speeds those drivers should be small.

Naturally, with bumpy track, we'll need some way of springing the drivers so that all of them are always in contact with the rails. And if we're going to get all those drivers, small though they are, around tight curves, the locomotive is going to have to be articulated. Naturally, any part of your engine that isn't contributing to tractive effort must be eliminated. In retrospect it would appear that the owners of the earliest logging roads chose to ignore all these features as they opted for off-the-shelf conventional rigid-frame rod locomotives, typically 4-4-0s, 2-6-0s, and later 2-8-0s.

The typical rod engine is a slippery and contentious machine. It is absolutely intolerant of bumpy track and will derail when confronted with any. Because of its rigid frame it will again derail on tight curves. The rigid frame also limited the number of drivers that could be used, regardless of size, so a rod engine was hard pressed to get even itself up a grade steeper than 4 percent, let alone hoist tonnage up a 5 percent one.

John Krause

Logging locomotives not only had to have tremendous adhesion, but had to be very flexible, as illustrated by this typical logging railroad track-laying operation on Elk River Coal & Lumber Co.'s line up the Lilly Fork in the early 1950s. No tie plates or ballast, and rough-cut log ties! With rails moved as soon as a timber stand was depleted, top train speeds of 15mph, and the geared locomotives' great flexibility, this type construction was sufficient to the need.

Logging train wrecks with rod locomotives were frequent and usually disastrous. And when the locomotives weren't leaving the track or running away they were stalling on all but the mildest grades. For this reason, although common-carrier railroads had by then been steam-powered for 40 years, logging operations of the 1870s were still dependent on horse-drawn trams.

Although logging company owners may have known something about railroading, they were primarily timbermen and thus victims in a seller's market for what Baldwin, Brooks, Porter, or Richmond Locomotive Works had to offer. And since they could sell all the rod engines they could manufacture, there was no incentive for the locomotive builders to develop an engine for the radical

W. Va. Collection, W. Va. University

This broadside of W. Va. Pulp & Paper Co. Shay No. 11 shows a 3-truck, 100-ton locomotive, larger than most Shays. The three vertical cylinders turned a line shaft which then turned the small geared drivers. The gearing plus the placement of all weight on the drivers helped give the Shay tremendous tractive power.

requirements of a logging railroad.

Actually, there were a few logging roads that did stay at least partially with conventional rod locomotives to the end, because of operating conditions. Cherry River Boom & Lumber—of which we will have more later—still operated a couple of slide-valve 2-8-2s in the 1950s, but that was because it hauled its own logs over the Baltimore & Ohio. And those few roads that survived long enough—Meadow River Lumber is one—bought diesels regardless of what sort of steam locomotives they used and for much the same reasons as their common carrier cousins.

It remained for one of the loggers' own, Ephraim Shay of Michigan, to develop a practical logging locomotive. The first commercially-produced Shay locomotive, with eight drivers, slide valves, and a vertical boiler, was built in 1880 by the Lima Machine Works of Lima, Ohio, forerunner of Lima Locomotive Works. (The inventor had built a few of his own lcomotives, some of which had but four drivers, before that date.)

Early Shays looked much like very early conventional locomotives in that they had upright boilers and eight wheels, although eventually the vast majority were built with horizontal boilers and the resultant locomotives looked much like ordinary rod engines of the time from the running board up, when the left side is viewed broadside.

What distinguished all but the smallest Shays, which had but two, were three vertical cylinders mounted on the right side of the boiler which necessitated shifting the entire boiler to the left to keep the locomotive balanced and to allow clearance for the cylinders. All Shays built by Lima used Stephenson valve gear. The cylinder pistons drove a flexible line shaft with universal couplings and slip joints through bevel gears. This flexibility allowed each individual truck to ride up and down on the lumpy track without regard to what its fellow trucks might be doing. Worthy of note is the fact that Lima continued to put slide valves on its Shays until the late-1920s, long after piston valves had become the standard on rod locomotives, and then used piston valves only in limited number of applications when forced to do so by competitors.

With the flexible line shaft and what were basically modified four-wheel freight car trucks, we have secured articulation on the roughest of track without the necessity of having any flexible joints in steam lines as was the case with conventional articulated rod locomotives. And depending on the number of trucks, we have 8, 12, or 16 small-diameter (typically 36-inch) drive wheels, giving the desired adhesion and tractive effort at low speeds. Since the use of a line shaft driven directly by the pistons eliminated the need for counter-balanced drivers, the problem of dynamic augment, or "hammer blow" on the rails was eliminated. Shays could traverse mugh lighter rail than could a rod locomotive with the same axle loading. It was those small wheels plus the three cylinders that were responsible for that small train in the introduction sounding like 50 mph when it was only doing 10.

Although it is not immediately obvious how (a partial reason with the Shay is the use of three cylinders and the gear ratio between the shaft and driver gears), the fluctations in torque and tractive effort per drive wheel revolution are less for a geared locomotive than for a conventional rod engine of comparable mean tractive effort and the same driver diameter and speed. This reduction in torque fluctuations further improves the adhesion and stalling characteristics of a geared locomotive. With a 2:1 gear ratio between the shaft and the drive gears, there were three times as many exhausts per drive wheel revolution as on a rod locomotive, which produced a steady draft at low speeds, and a Shay had excellent steaming qualities.

Because a Shay was seldom far from fuel and water, a small coal bunker behind the cab plus a water tender connected behind the bunker by means of a drawbar ordinarily sufficed. In the case of two-truck Shays coal and water were carried in the same tender. A really big tender held 9 tons of coal and 8,000 gallons of water. More typically, capacities were in the order of 5 tons and 3,000 gallons of water for a 70-ton Shay.

With the rearmost truck or set of drivers under the water tender, all parts of the Shay were contributing to tractive effort. And with every wheel connected to every other wheel via the line shaft or axles, no wheel of a Shay could slip unless they all slipped. All drivers did slip sometimes. Ice or snow on the rails would do it. And Cass residents used to tell the tale (apophrycal perhaps) of one of Mower Lumber Company's Shays stalling when a horde of grasshoppers settled on the rails. But bad weather and grasshoppers aside, slipping was infrequent. By comparison, an engineer on a conventional articulated trying to accelerate his train too rapidly could find his forward drivers spinning wildly while the rear ones were struggling to turn.

Most standard gauge Shays after 1920 were the three-truck type (the narrow gauge variety were still double-truckers), typically with one truck just behind the pilot beam, the second below the cab or coal bunker, and the third under the water tender. Some exceptions were four-truckers built for mine switching operations of the Chesapeake & Ohio Railway in West Virginia. One three-truck locomotive, a 150-ton behemoth owned by Greenbrier Cheat & Elk (a Cass Scenic Railroad predecessor) was subsequently converted to four trucks. Shays were usually classified according to the number of cylinders and trucks as follows:

Class	Trucks	Cylinders
A	2	2
B	2	3
C	3	3
D	4	3

The Shay was the total logging transportation machine; typically weighing between 50 and 100 tons, it could go anywhere, pull almost anything, and was perfectly at ease on the rudest of tracks. In fact, it is said that a Shay engineer driving his engine at night

Charles E. Winters

The Climax was the second most popular of the geared logging locomotives. Here Elk River Coal & Lumber Company's No. 3 Climax and its crew take a rest near Dundon in the spring of 1955. The Climax's canted cylinders transmitted their power to its drivers by means of a gearing mechanism that was not as obvious as the Shay's. - The wire spark arrester atop the stack was an important feature for logging engines, working as they did in the sometimes highly combustible woods.

could always tell if the engine had derailed—the ride suddenly got smoother! To allay customer fear of what problems would arise if a Shay did derail, Lima advertising modestly proclaimed that "It is unusual to require the assistance of another engine to help a Shay on to the track after derailment." In other words, they pulled themselves back on the track. No wonder Lima continued to produce Shays until 1945.

Some idea of the staying power of this mechanical marvel lies in the fact that of the 2,771 Shays built since 1880 for use in North America and around the world, at least 84 still exist, of which 27 are known to be either in service or considered servicable. Of these, 16 are from West Virginia logging roads. If rod engines had survived proportionately and only locomotives built after 1900 are considered, we'd have almost 850 in service, whereas the actual number today is less than one third that.

Nobody's happy with perfection, however, and it was not long before competitors appeared on the market. The first of these, the Climax, brainchild of inventor Charles D. Scott, was first built by the Climax Machinery Company of Corry, Pennsylvania, in 1884.

If the Shay had an Achilles heel that could be exploited by other designs, it was the complex flexible line shaft and bevel gears that required an inordinate amount of maintenance and lubrication. Fortunately, a Shay's gears and line shaft were out in the open where they were easy to work on. A secondary drawback was that stuffing the cylinders next to the boiler limited the boiler size.

You would be excused the logical assumption that Climax would have tried to break into the logging locomotive market by eliminating Shay's drawbacks while avoiding any new ones of its own. To a certain extent Climax did neither. However, the Climax was inexpensive to purchase and, despite the fact that the gearing was beneath the boiler, relatively easy to maintain.

Railroad Museum of Pennsylvania

This spiffy little 36-inch gauge Heisler was once the pride and joy of Pardee & Curtin Lumber Co., the largest narrow gauge logger in West Virginia in the 1920s. The Heisler's inward slanting "V" cylinders are very evident in this photo.

Climax employed two cylinders, one on each side of the boiler and either Stephenson or Walschaerts valve gear. The cylinders were neither vertical nor horizontal. Rather they were inclined longitudinally at an angle of approximately 25 degrees and the piston rods were connected to a line shaft centered under the boiler and midway between the trucks (Climaxes were all either two-or three-truck designs). These trucks had dimensions and physical characteristics approximating those of a conventional freight car. The line shaft in turn powered both axles on each truck.

Whatever advantages the Climax may have possessed were mostly lost on the average lumber baron. Production ended just before the Great Depression and never resumed. Of the 1,100* or so built, only 18 have survived intact, including four in New Zealand, and three, all West Virginia logging alumni, are known to be operational. Most standard gauge Climaxes weighed an average of 40 to 90 tons. Only one Climax weighed as much as 100 tons.

Perhaps it would seem that by 1892 any locomotive builder would have been smart enough not to compete with Lima's Shays. But that year mechanical engineer Charles L. Heisler received a patent on his own version of a geared locomotive. In 1894 the Stearns Manufacturing Company of Erie, Pennsylvania, began several reorganizations and emerged in 1907 as the Heisler Locomotive Works.

Although the Heisler employed a frame structure similar to that of the Shay, it was much closer to the Climax both in appearance and in construction. To the casual train watcher, the most obvious difference between the Heisler and Climax was that the Heisler's cylinders were slanted inward at a 45-degree angle on either side of the boiler so that the angle between their piston rods was 90 degrees. Stephenson valve gear was standard.

The pistons were directly connected to a line shaft located between the trucks and the line shaft drove the far axles through bevel gears. Heislers employed either two or three trucks. The spoked wheels in each truck were side-rod connected and counterbalanced, so there were but three sets of bevel gears, at most, to cause mischief. Weights customarily varied from 40 to 80 tons, for standard gauge Heislers, although twelve 90-ton Heslers were built.

If you accept the Heisler Works' press release as gospel, the Heisler was quite a puller. One healthy 65-tonner reputedly hauled 580 loads over an 8-mile track in May 1923. If you figure 25 working days in a 1923 month with no down time, this locomotive was hauling an average of 23 cars a day. And that year, a smallish 36-tonner muscled 524 loaded cars out of the woods over a seven-mile track in just 20 working days. Just where these locomotives were performing these feats is not known but even if they were operating in gradeless Louisiana bayous, the figures are impressive.

Heisler built 850* locomotives before the last one was outshopped in 1941. Of that number, 32 are known to have survived and 11, including 2 from West Virginia, are considered operational.

It should be noted in passing that the Shay, Climax, and Heisler were not the only geared logging engines ever built, Willamette and Baldwin being two of the better known minor-league logging engine builders. The three majors were, howerver, virtually the only types employed in West Virginia.

These numbers are from Steam & Thunder In the Timber, *by Michael Koch (World Press, New York 1979). Alfred W. Bruce, in his* Steam Locomotives of North America *(W. W. Norton & Co., New York, 1952), states that 500 Climaxes and 850 Heislers were built.* The Climax Locomotive *by Thomas Tabor (1960) also states that 1,100 Climaxes were constructed. Klein's* The Heisler Locomotive *(1982) lists 625 Heislers. We cannot account for these disparate numbers but are inclined to go with Koch's figures.*

Thomas Lawson, Jr. Coll.

Uncommon in logging was the standard rod locomotive used in almost all other railroading. In West Virginia, Cherry River Boom and Lumber Company was the largest logger using rod locomotives. Here a 2-8-2 Mikado type with seemingly tiny drivers poses at Richwood in August 1956. It appears that No. 15 is getting ready to tote some empty logging flats to one of the company's logging camps.

W. Va. Coll., W. Va. University

An impressive show of Shay power at West Virginia Pulp & Paper Company's Spruce, W.Va. engine house about 1904, includes (left-to right) Nos. 3, 2, 1 and 4. The locomotives were almost brand new when this photo was taken.

The Shay Geared Locomotive - Components

1 *Cylinder*
2 *Exhaust Pipe*
3 *Exhaust Pipe Elbow*
4 *Exhaust Reducer*
5 *Line Shaft*
6 *Right Truck Box Cap*
7 *Gear*
8 *Coupling Ring*
9 *Square Shaft*
10 *Sleeve Coupling*
11 *Crank Shaft*
12 *Crank Box Cap*
13 *Cylinder Frame*
14 *Tumbling Shaft*
15 *Truss Rod End, Back*
16 *Truss Rod End, Front*
17 *Reverse Lever Shaft Arm*
18 *Coal Bunk*
19 *Water Tank*
20 *Rear Sand Box*

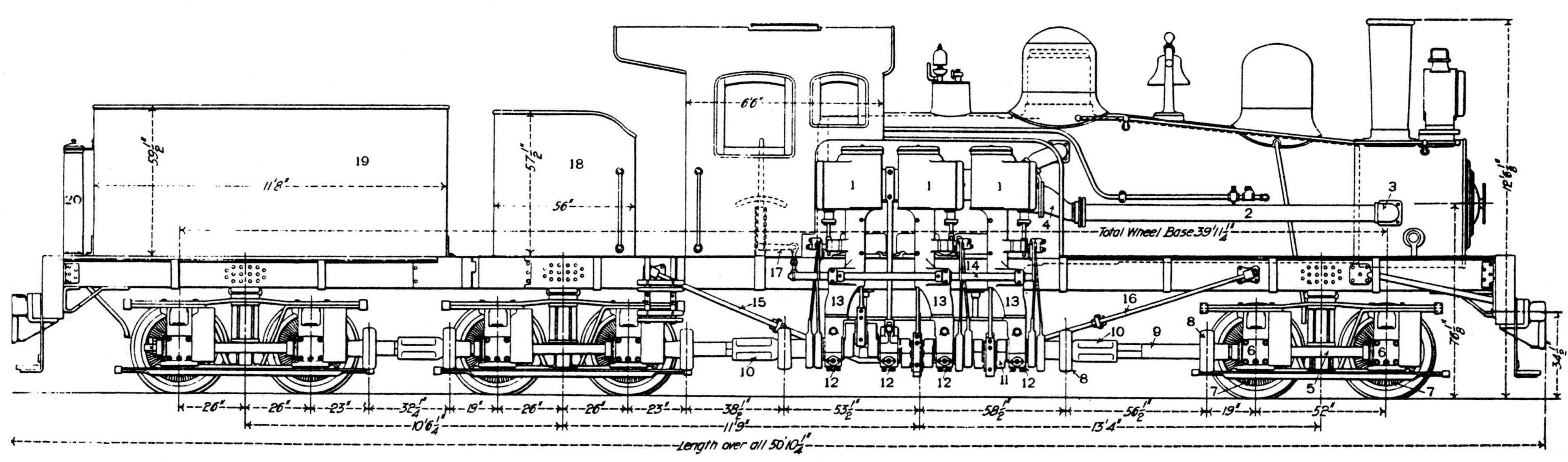

Of the three major types of geared locomotives, the Shay was by far the most popular nationally, and in West Virginia. Manufactured exclusively by the Lima Locomotive Works, in Lima, Ohio, the Shay was used mainly in logging operations, but some were also used for industrial switching and even some major railroads employed them on lines with steep grades and heavy loads, most notably the Chesapeake & Ohio (in West Virginia, it might be added) and the Southern. In West Virginia over 200 Shays were used in logging, although the Climax type comes in second with about 150 recorded in the state, while the Heisler runs a distant third with only about 20 examples in the West Virginia hills. — This drawing shows the design and arrangement of a typical three-truck Shay. Most striking is the vertical arrangement of three cylinders on one side of the boiler. The small coal bunker directly behind the cab was separate from the water tank which followed, but everything contributed to the weight on the drivers and thus the tractive power of the locomotive.

The Heisler Locomotive - Typical Arrangement

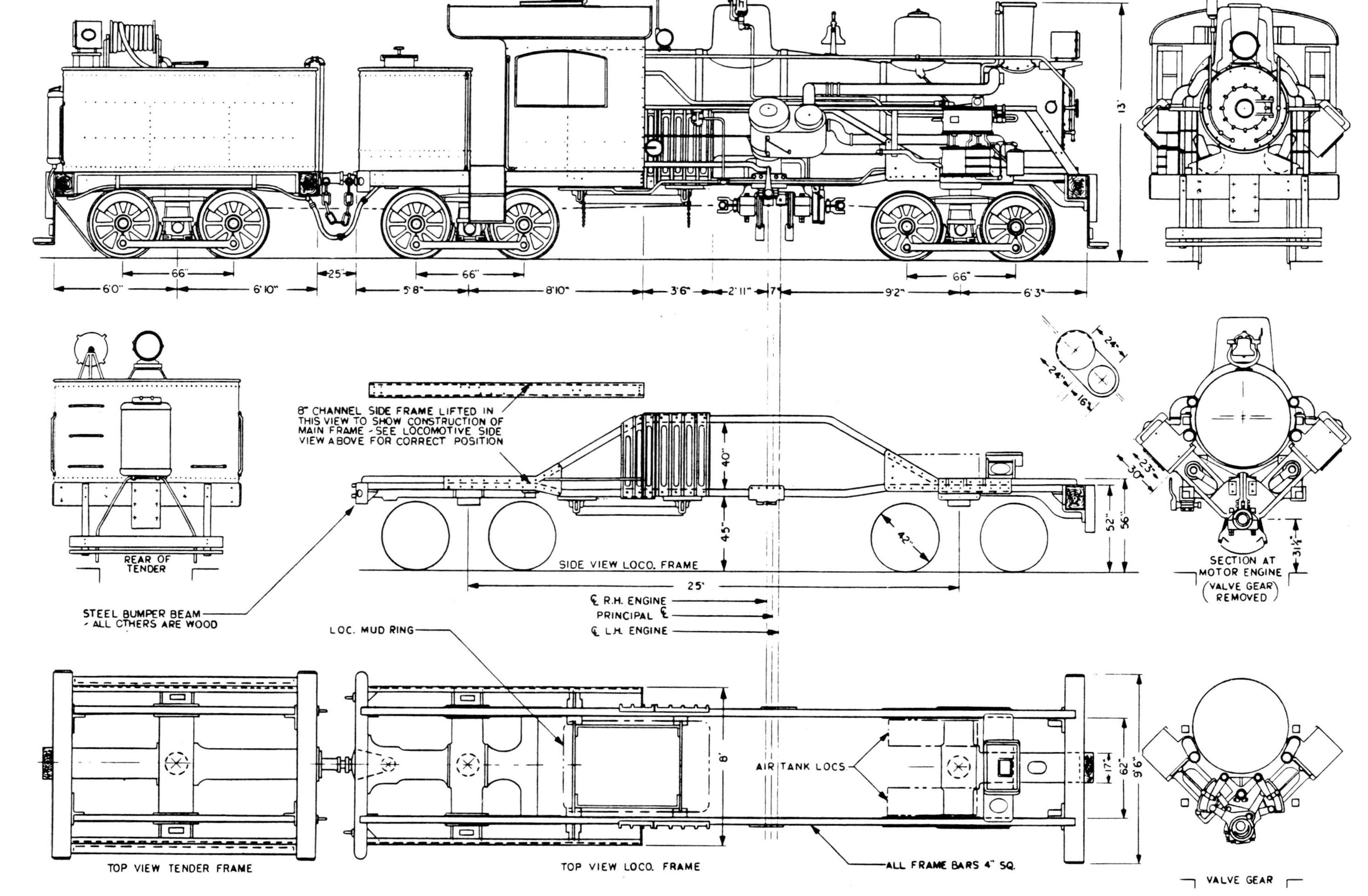

From *The Heisler Locomotive* by B. F. G. Klein

These drawings show an elevation of a typical large three-truck Heisler and below that a view of its frame, while a plan view is presented at the bottom. End elevations and sections at the cylinders are also shown, the latter giving an excellent depiction of the "V" cylinder alignment. Heislers were built between 1891 and 1941, and were a distant third in the race for supremacy in logging railroads. The most reliable figures indicate about 625 were built.

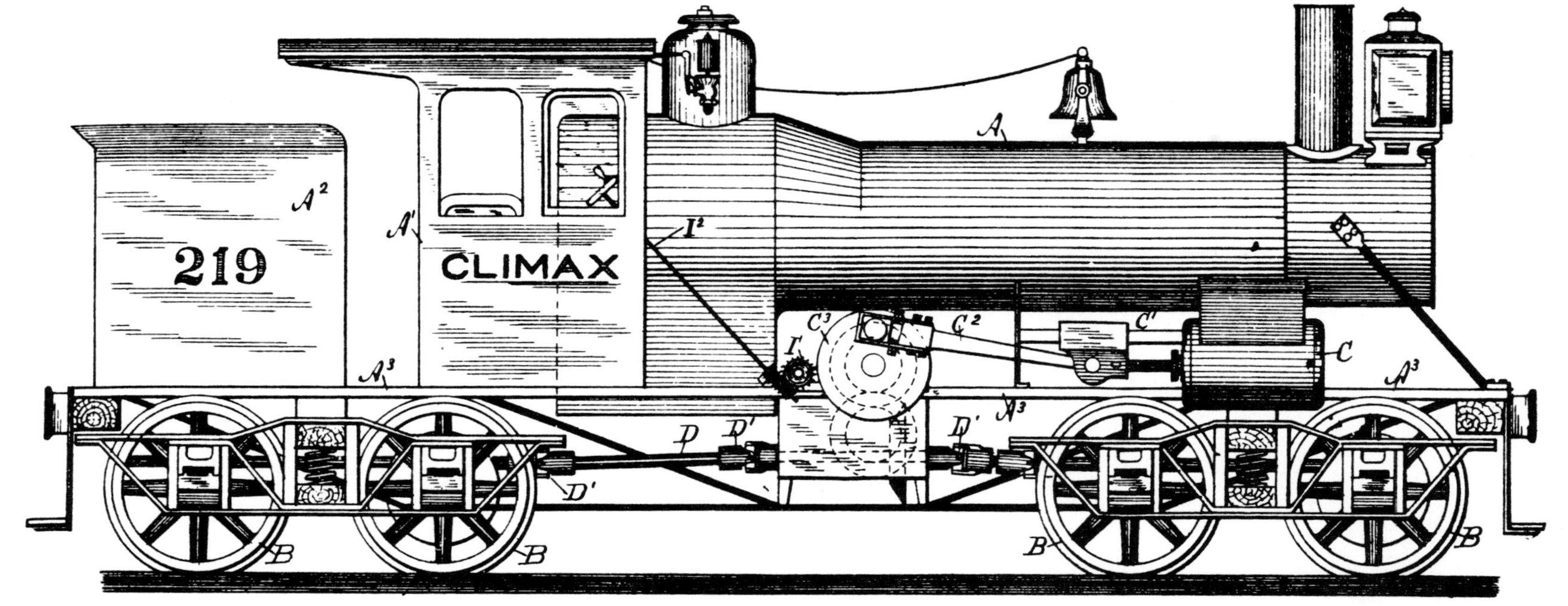

Mechanical drawings of the Climax type are hard to find. This patent drawing shows an early version of the locomotive, with the cylinders placed horizontally. Production models had the angled cylinders so that the drive shaft and its gearing mechanisms could be located well below the boiler. The smaller drawing is a representation of the Climax's drive shaft showing its gear connections to the wheels. Of course the great advantage of any of the geared locomotives was that they could generate great tractive power and adhesion because all their wheels were drivers. This allowed the use of the entire weight of the locomotive and its fuel to increase traction. The drivers were powered by gears, which were thus less prone to slip than conventional rod locomotives.

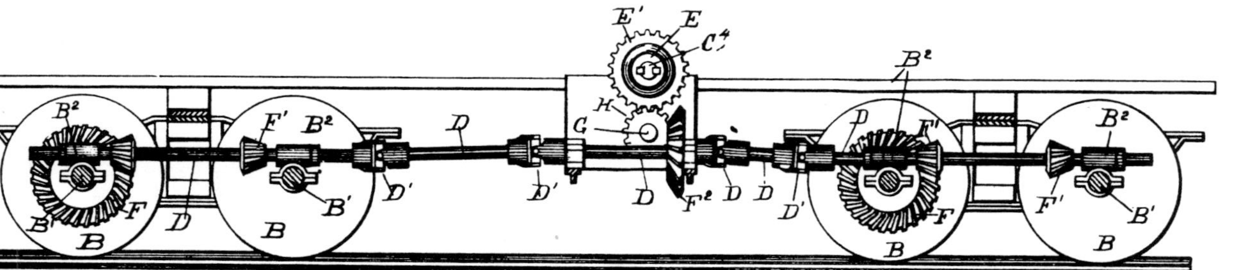

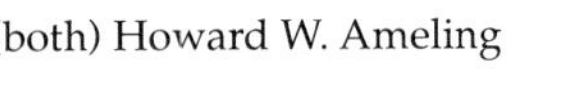
(both) Howard W. Ameling

(Upper left) This rendering is taken from an 1899 Climax advertisement showing a typical locomotive as would have been used in West Virginia operations. Climaxes tended to be on the smaller side, with many two-truck engines in use. ***(Upper right)*** A close-up of W. M. Ritter Lumber Company Climax No. 3's builder plate in June 1962, shows it to be Shop or Construction Serial No. 1692, and lists patents dated 1880 through 1892. ***(Lower right)*** Ritter Climax No. 3 back in the deep woods in September 1958, the engineer looking to the rear for a signal to back up with his single flat car.

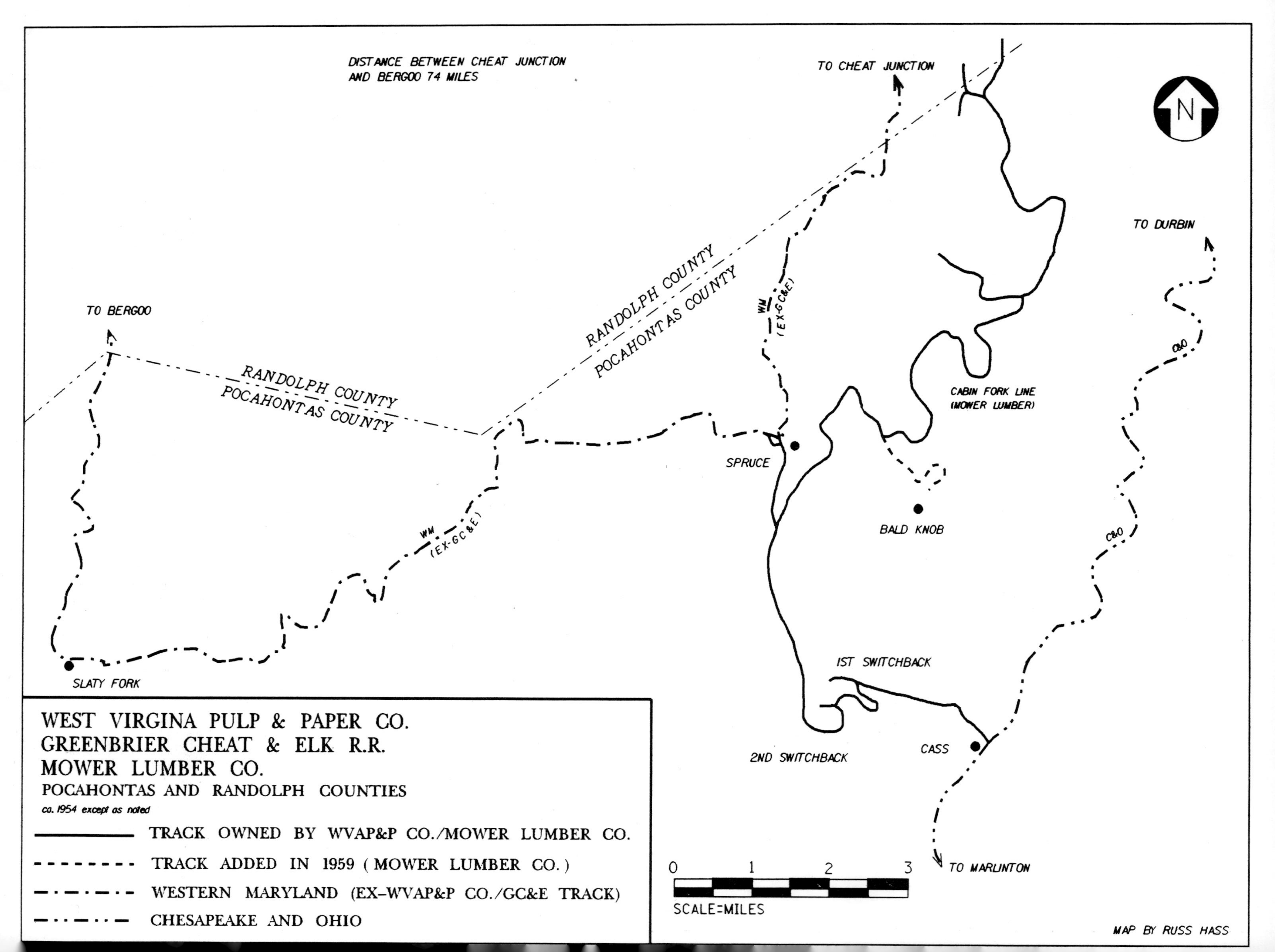

WEST VIRGINA PULP & PAPER CO.
GREENBRIER CHEAT & ELK R.R.
MOWER LUMBER CO.
POCAHONTAS AND RANDOLPH COUNTIES
co. 1954 except as noted
TRACK OWNED BY WVAP&P CO./MOWER LUMBER CO.
TRACK ADDED IN 1959 (MOWER LUMBER CO.)
WESTERN MARYLAND (EX-WVAP&P CO./GC&E TRACK)
CHESAPEAKE AND OHIO
DISTANCE BETWEEN CHEAT JUNCTION
AND BERGOO 74 MILES
TO CHEAT JUNCTION
N
TO BERGOO
RANDOLPH COUNTY
POCAHONTAS COUNTY
RANDOLPH COUNTY
POCAHONTAS COUNTY
WM
(EX-GC&E)
WM
(EX-GC&E)
SPRUCE
CABIN FORK LINE
(MOWER LUMBER)
BALD KNOB
TO DURBIN
C&O
C&O
SLATY FORK
IST SWITCHBACK
2ND SWITCHBACK
CASS
TO MARLINTON
0
1
2
3
SCALE=MILES
MAP BY RUSS HASS

Chapter 3 — Mower Lumber Company— West Virginia Pulp & Paper Company (Cass, Pocahontas County)

Between June 1899 and December 1903, the Greenbrier Railway Company built a line up the Greenbrier River valley from Whitcomb on the Chesapeake & Ohio main line, through Cass, to a connection with the Coal and Iron Railway (which became part of the Western Maryland in 1905) at Durbin, thus opening almost unexplored woodland along the valley to loggers. The Greenbrier Railway was a wholy owned subsidiary of the C&O and was absorbed into that road in 1903 as its Greenbrier Division (later subdivision). The line was built at the instigation of the West Virginia Pulp and Paper Company which planned a large paper mill to be built near North Caldwell, about four miles up the branch from Whitcomb. This mill was actually located at Covington, Virginia, about 30 miles east on the C&O main line and is still in operation there.

Logging existed in the valley before 1902 and some spectacular log drives from the late 1880s have been recorded. But floating logs down the Greenbrier to Ronceverte was expensive and it was impractical to really go back into the deep mountains for timber.

While the Greenbrier's tracks were being laid, West Virginia Pulp & Paper Co., through a subsidiary, West Virginia Spruce Lumber Co., bought some 173,000 acres up the mountain from Cass—named for West Virginia Pulp & Paper Vice President Joseph K. Cass. The firm built a company store where a mill hand could purchase anything from an ice cream soda to plumbing supplies, and a band mill—at one time reputedly the largest double-band mill in the world—and laid out a logging railroad to bring out the red spruce pulpwood and hardwood logs. Despite this ambitious planning, West Virginia Spruce's first locomotive at Cass was a modest-size 2-truck, 42-ton Shay, No. 1(some sources call this a 40-ton locomotive).

The new road was christened the Greenbrier & Elk River Railroad. This name was changed to Greenbrier, Cheat & Elk in 1910 and it operated as a common carrier until 1928.

Incidentally, one of West Virginia Spruce's early customers was the Wright Cycle Company of Dayton, Ohio, whose proprietors, brothers Wilbur and Orville

Some idea of the size of the first mill at Cass and the loading dock can be gathered from this photo taken about 1915. The box cars are on the Chesapeake & Ohio Railway's Greenbrier branch, built to accommodate the huge Cass operation as well as many other mills that sprang up along the 101-mile line following the Greenbrier River.

Westvaco photo, W. P. McNeel Coll.

This photo shows the pond of the original Cass mill. Judging from the number of loaded log flats arriving, this was a very busy day. Cars at right are loaded with pulpwood for the WVaP&P's huge paper mill at Covington, Virginia, 121 miles distant via the C&O.

mill rode in some of these trains. Interspersed with the logging trains was an occasional trainload of supplies for the logging camps and track crews. (Logging camps were usually numbered in succession as built, although early on the numbers sometimes followed the loggers as they moved from site to site. Camp number 9, for example, might be five miles removed today from where it was a month before.) In terms of train movements, Greenbrier Cheat & Elk's rails were as busy as the main line of some modern-day class I railroads.

A fire that destroyed the band mill, planning mill, and storage house in February 1922 slowed expansion only momentarily. By the mid-1920s West Virginia Pulp & Paper was running one of the largest logging operations ever in the state.

Wright, ordered "500 feet of the finest possible spruce for use in constructing flying machines." The brothers, of course, were the inventors of the first successful airplane.

Expansion was rapid. By 1917, the GC&E had over 66 miles of track in operation. By 1921 that figure was 101 miles and Pocahontas County's population peaked at 15,002 (1990 population was down to 9,008). The rails struggled up Leatherbark Run, skirted 4,842-foot Bald Knob, the state's second highest peak, and split at the pulp mill hamlet of Spruce, where one branch—sold to Western Maryland Railway in 1928 and powered by WM 0-6-0s and 2-8-0s—headed west to Bergoo near Webster Springs. The other line, also sold to the Western Maryland Railway in 1928, followed Shavers Fork north into Randolph County and eventually connected with the Western Maryland. WVaP&P retained trackage rights over these branches on a per-car and per-engine basis. GC&E Shays even hauled WM coal trains for a while. Eleven Shays, ranging in size from 2-truck, 42-ton No. 1, to No. 12, a 154-ton 3-truck behemoth purchased in 1921 and converted in the 1930s to a 4-truck locomotive weighing 192 (or 197 depending on whose data you accept) tons smoked and blew their mellow whistles through the woods, and 1,500 men cut logs. Two ex-C&O 4-truck Shays joined the roster in 1923.

Steam-operated Lidgerwood skidders and teams of horses moved the logs to the rail flat cars and Barnhart log loaders piled them on—60 cars a day on the average, six days a week in the 1920s. Since a good trainload would be 10 to 13 cars, an average of six log trains a day rolled out of the woods. Chesapeake & Ohio pulpwood racks destined for West Virginia Pulp & Paper's Covington

The constant taking up and re-laying of track to reach new timber stands kept 30 section crews busy. Composed of Poles, Czechs, Hungarians, Italians, and Austrians, the crews were brought into Cass by the boxcar—use of day coaches was unthinkable—and Cass, in common with other lumber towns in the state, became a polyglot community. Since spelling and pronunciation of these foreign names was beyond the ken of most native-born supervisors, the foreigners were usually designated by numbers for paycheck and record-keeping purposes, and a paycheck would be made out to "Italian No. 3" or "Hungarian No. 6." According to some reports, the workers were simply given numbers, without regard to nationality, so a paycheck might read simply "No. 6."

Unlike many of the locals, the foreigners were a frugal and sobersided lot and paydays found them at the local post office mailing money home. But the nomadic "wood hicks," the men who did the actual logging, were fiercely independent men of mostly Scotch-Irish ancestry. Their appetites for hard liquor and soft women, gambling and fighting were legendary.

For these men, Cass became a roaring company town on Saturday nights, a "subdivision of hell," one writer dubbed it. Liquor and blood flowed with equal ease in the little town. It is said that by the 1920s, Cass averaged a murder a month, and the going price for having an enemy killed was $7.50, or about a day's pay. [This may be a bit of hyperbole; West Virginia author Warren Blackhurst once suggested to this writer that the average was three or four murders a year. In either case, Cass was not a model of decorum and propriety.]

All the blood shed locally wasn't flowing just on

Saturday night. With GC&E grades ranging up to 11 percent, runaways were frequent, although not necessarily fatal. For example, take the time that veteran engineer George "Piney" Williams was at the throttle when his Shay left the rails. Piney was never seen without his corncob pipe—although it was against company policy to smoke on the property—and derailments were no exception. When the dust settled, the stunned engineer was found unhurt. The bowl of the pipe was missing; however, the stem was still clenched in his teeth.

None of the other communities that sprang up along the GC&E reached the size or the notoriety of Cass. Raucous Spruce did gain a touch of fame locally for the large number of hunters who rode in on the logging cars from Cass, and for the depths of the snows that accumulated at its 3,853-foot elevation. One particularly noteworthy snowfall started at 6:00 a.m. on December 7, 1944, and there were 36 inches of the stuff on the ground by 11:30 a.m. By the end of the third day, snow was up to the second floor of the Spruce boarding house.

That time three Shays were called out of the Cass engine house to conquer the drifts. Walter Good was engineer on the lead engine and he reported that snow came in the cab window so badly the plowing operation had to be halted to shovel it out. It was a full week before the track was open past Spruce, and the boarding house, which had room for 14, slept 22 people, two of them women, that week.

No stand of pulpwood, particularly in areas where reforestation is not practiced, lasts forever and the pulp and paper company's stand near Cass finally played out just after the start of World War II, leaving the firm little reason to remain in the logging business. But there was considerable hardwood and second-growth spruce below Bald Knob and that same year West Virginia Pulp & Paper Company sold the entire Cass operation to F. Edwin Mower (the first syllable rhymes with "cow"), head of the Charleston-based Mower Lumber Company. Thereafter the legend on the Shay's flanks read "Mower Lumber Company."

Stands of hardwood are not inexhaustable either. By 1960 Mower Lumber had retrenched to 65,000 acres (with most of the remaining West Virginia Pulp & Paper land now part of the Monongahela National Forest), 12 miles of track terminating at Bald Knob (which the railroad had reached only the previous year by building a short branch off the Cabin Fork line), three Shays, and three trains a week. The 11 percent grades and two switchbacks were still in place and a logging train going to Bald Knob from Cass had to make a stop along the way at a creek-filled tank to fill up the tender. Mill machinery was generally considered to be either worn out or obsolete.

Edwin Mower had died four years earlier and a younger brother, Donald, made president. Just what happened next seems open to dispute. According to one version Edwin's wife, Dorothy, through stock ownership, still controlled the remains of the fast-crumbling lumber empire and she wanted to liquidate. Mower family members, however, have stoutly maintained that Dorothy had nothing to do with Mower Lumber's demise.

Feelings against Mrs. Mower reportedly ran high in Pocahontas County. There were still several hundred loggers, mill hands, and railroaders on the payroll, and

Westvaco photo, W. P. McNeel Coll.

The second mill at Cass, replacing the one burned in 1922, with the peaceful Greenbrier River in the foreground, probably about 1940. The mill structure lasted to the end of logging at Cass, lay derelict for many years after the tourist line started operation, and finally burned in comparatively recent times.

aside from the National Science Foundation's radio telescope erected at nearby Green Bank in 1959 and a small tannery at Frank, there was no other industry in the area. The spectre of mass unemployment hung over the upper Greenbrier Valley.

Mrs. Mower had her way, it appears, and the property was sold to Walworth Farms, a subsidiary of shipping and chemical conglomerate W. R. Grace & Co. In a mega-corporation such as Grace, small matters like the viability of a remote logging empire are apt to get overlooked initially. It did not take long, however, for word to filter up to the CEO.

Walworth soon determined that it would be uneconomical to extend the lumber railroad's 85-pound steel into what was left of the timber stand, and operations were abandoned on June 30, 1960. In September 1960, the remnants of the railroad were sold to Midwest Raleigh Steel Corporation, a Kanawha County, West Virginia used railroad material dealer, and the dismantling process began. Railroad equipment was lettered "Midwest Raleigh" briefly.

By rights, our story should end here and if it did the WVaP&P/Mower Lumber Co. railroad would hardly make the lead story of this book. But the logging railroad was to be reincarnated in a form that would bring it far more fame (if not fortune, too) than it ever knew in its lumbering days.

The economic collapse of just another small West Virginia valley town was so commonplace in 1960 that news of such seldom reached the outside world. Thus, Sunbury, Pennslyvania sporting goods dealer Russell C. Baum was unprepared for the sight of scrappers tearing up his favorite logging railroad when he opted for a three-day vacation in Pocahontas County in October 1960.

Checking into Bill Sperry's El Poca Motel in Marlinton, 40 miles to the south, Baum communicated his grief to Sperry, pointing out to the motel operator the tourist potential and historical significance of the railroad. "Russ," replied Sperry, "I know the man to talk to—Jim Comstock, editor of the *West Virginia Hillbilly* over in Richwood. He's a man that can get things done. Let's see him tonight."

Baum had traveled several hundred miles since 3:00 a.m. that day. It was now 7:00 p.m., and the prospect of a 100-mile round trip to Richwood left him faint. However, he was game and the trip was made. In Richwood, Comstock listened attentively to Baum's plea and then asked Baum to meet him in the Capitol in Charleston the next day to talk with State Delegate J. C. Cruikshank. Baum agreed.

Impressed with the railfan's story of the Cass area's plight, Cruikshank requested and got a 24-hour recess of the West Virginia Legislature. He then prevailed upon the Pennsylvanian—who had planned to spend his last vaction day photographing W. M. Ritter Lumber Company steam at Swandale and Avoca—to address the lawmakers.

Baum presented his case and in a voice vote that was far from unanimous, the legislature agreed to appoint a committee to investigate the possibilities of turning the Mower railroad into a tourist attraction. A committee known as the Cass Planning Commission was formed to save the railroad. Led by P. F. "Bus" Long, C&O agent at Cass, and Jack Kane, Cass grocer, the commission appealed to Midwest Raleigh Steel President Sam Silverstein to suspend the track dismantling operation temporarily. Silverstein, who had already removed some track, agreed to this and the legislature began its investigation.

To say the solons of economically depressed West Virginia were unenthusiastic about their state going into the speculative business of operating a tourist railroad would be an understatement. Tourist railroads in 1960 were still largely untried and the cash-strapped Mountain State had been seeing its tax base steadily erode for almost 15 years. However, on October 23, 1960, the legislative committee appeared at Cass. They rode up the slope of Back Allegheny Mountain behind one of the smoke-belching Shays and dined in the camp cars. Returning to Charleston, the committee recommended that the state acquire the railroad.

By now it was January 1961. There was a new Governor, W. W. Barron, plus many new legislators in office, 1960 having been an election year. The newcomers were even more opposed to their state operating a railroad than had been their precedessors.

John P. Killoran

On October 23, 1960, the powerful Government & Finance Committee of the West Virginia Legislature toured the Mower Lumber Co. to evaluate its potential as a tourist railroad. Included in the photo are Cass C&O agent Bus Long (second left seated) and editor Jim Comstock (seated second from right), as well as the president of Mower Lumber, and President Ted Riffe of the Cass Planning Commission.

Delegate Cruikshank then visited Barron and, as he later put it "...talked to him about our heritage in strong language." The new governor agreed to look at the railroad and in the legislature Cruikshank introduced House Concurrant Resolution No. 17, "Directing the Directors of the Conservation Commission to purchase the logging railroad and rolling stock...used by the Mower

Lumber Company in its logging operation at Cass." The resolution was adopted March 7, 1961.

After much skullduggery, log rolling, and legal—and some say, extralegal—maneuvering in the big Capitol overlooking the Kanawha River, the legislators appropriated $150,000 for purchase of the road, rolling stock, and 40 acres of Gum Field (now Whittaker Station) on Back Allegheny Mountain for the road's terminus. It also directed that the line be turned over to the Department of Natural Resources to operate. An additional $40,000 was later appropriated for the acquisition of the Cass maintenance shop and equipment. Cass had been hauled back from death's door.

On April 23, 1961, the town turned out *en masse* to watch Western Maryland ALCO diesel No. 193 trundle two silver-roofed passenger cars into Cass with the governor and state media representatives. It was the first passenger train into Cass since 1958 when the C&O ceased its daily motor car train. The train came from Elkins, the governor's home town, and had transferred to the C&O at Durbin. Shays No. 1 and No. 4 were fired up and the governor and his party went clanking up the mountain. Barron was favorably impressed.

But $190,000 didn't go far even back in 1961 and the Cass Planning Commission was determined to get a few necessities for free. The C&O had just concluded its annual stockholder's meeting at White Sulphur Springs' posh Greenbrier resort hotel when Cass station agent Long accosted gruff C&O Vice President M. I. Dunn. Long had a sizeable shopping list of goodies he wanted the Chessie Route to donate to the Cass road. Before the two men departed, the persuasive Long had conned his boss out of two thirds of the Cass depot, trackage rights from the depot to the start of the ex-logging road trackage, the water tank, and three vintage C&O coaches. Dunn also agreed to supply a Clifton Forge shop crew to handle overhaul of the neglected Shays.

A hero of the Cass Scenic Railroad was C&O agent P. F. Long, shown here in 1964 dispensing tickets to tourists for the ride up the mountain from the C&O station office. Paneling in the office was cut by Mower Lumber.

The arduous job of putting what was to become today's famed Cass Scenic Railroad on its feet—or its rails—started. When Department of Natural Resources officials recovered from the shock of finding themselves cast in the role of railroad executives, they appointed Ben Dickens, a West Virginia University forestry graduate, as the Cass Scenic Railroad's temporary superintendent. Dickens, who had been assistant superintendent of West Virginia's Lost River State Park before coming to Cass, later admitted to not having known a cylinder head from a Johnson bar before tackling the job. " don't know if I was sent to help the railroad or bog it down completely," he laughed. Dickens and his men did a remarkable job. Given $10,000 for the initial year's operation before the very first trainload of paying passengers was pushed up the mountain from Cass on June 15, 1963, they had spent that amount in three months.

In the first season the Cass Scenic Railroad carried 23,106 passengers; 36,523 made the trip in 1964, and the number has increased most years since. In May 1968, the track was opened all the way to Bald Knob with West Virginia Governor Hulett Smith driving the golden spike (See page 42) and vistors today are treated to a 25-mile panoramic view of forested mountains marching eastward to the horizon.

And as you gaze out on this scenic wonder, give a thought to the disparate group of men whose effort made it possible: There was the sporting goods salesman and a motel operator, a grocer, a newspaper editor, a state senator and a governor, a station agent and his big boss, and—maybe most important of all—a considerate scrap metal dealer. If Sam Silverstein had just said "no" at one critical point instead of "yes," Cass, the railroad, and its Shays would all have passed into history more than three decades ago.

(Right) Thanks to the Cass Scenic Railroad scenes like this have not passed into history, but are repeated daily during the summer season each year.

(both) William E. Warden

Logs splash into the mill pond at Cass as two workers watch from a gangway, ready to hustle the logs into the jack slip, seen at the center, which hoists them into the sawing room of the mill. This is the second Cass mill, built in 1922 after fire destroyed the original plant. Fire was always a great danger in lumbering operations—in the forests and among the wooden structures of the mills and towns.

Westvaco photo, W. P. McNeel Coll.

W. Va. Coll., W. Va. University

West Virginia Pulp & Paper Co. Shay No. 3 is lettered "Greenbrier & Elk River Railroad" amid the debris and confusion of logging in the 1905-10 period. The log loader working at the right is lettered "West Virginia Pulp & Paper." No. 3 was a three-truck 70-ton locomotive purchased new in 1903.

Shay No. 8 came to WVaP&P in 1912 and weighed 100 tons. It's large size is evident in this photo with a log train at the Spruce coal tipple about 1918. The crew in typical garb pose in the classic demeanor of railroaders, be they loggers or mainliners.

(both) W. Va. Coll., W. Va. University

Shay No. 10 was a 70-ton three-trucker built by Lima in 1914. No. 10 was sold to R. E. Wood Lumber Co. in 1926 and became their No. 1698, and then two years later in 1928 it went to The Sound Timber Company in Washington State. The crew looks like they'd rather be doing almost anything than having their picture made, but people of that era seldom smiled in photos.

Harold A. Hill photo; Thomas Lawson, Jr. Coll.

Far from its original home, No. 10 is the property of The Sound Timber Company of Darrington, Washington (its No. 3) in this photo and will have one more owner before being scrapped in 1950. Note the elaborate spark arrester laying on the sand dome. Photographed in 1937.

Another logging train poses with W. Va. Pulp & Paper Company's 80-ton Shay No. 5. The picture was probably taken at either Cass or Spruce about 1915. No. 5 was an 80-ton locomotive, built in 1905 for Cass. It remained in service throughout the Mower period and today still operates carrying tourists on the Cass Scenic Railroad.

(both) W. Va. Coll., W. Va. University

No date or locale is given on this photo of Shay No. 3, but it was probably taken before World War I. The engineer has his oil can out and the fireman a wrench in his hand, probably for tightening gear and shaft connections. No. 3 was a 70-tonner scrapped in the early 1930s.

Time has almost run out for Mower Lumber Co. Shay No. 1, waiting silently under the Cass coal tipple in July 1959. But No. 1 will rise phoenix-like from the ashes of the lumber company to haul tourists to the summit of Bald Knob. Ultimately it was traded to the B&O Railroad Museum for use of Western Maryland Shay No. 6. — No. 1 was built in 1905 for G. W. Huntley Lumber Company, was owned by Flint & Stoner Lumber and then by North Fork Lumber, which traded it to WVaP&P for their first No. 1, a much lighter 2-truck 42-tonner, in 1915.

William E. Warden

Locomotives of W. Va. Pulp & Paper Co./Mower Lumber Co.

No.	Type	Date Built	BP(psi)	Driver size	Cylinder size/stroke	C/N	Previous Owners
1(1st)	Shay/2-truck-42-ton	1900	145	29.5	11x12	630	Purchased new by W. Va. Spruce Lbr. - lettered "Greenbrier & Elk River RR"
1(2nd)	Shay/3-truck-65-ton	1905	200	36	12x15	1519	G. W. Huntley Lbr. Flint Erving & Stoner Lbr. North Fork Lbr. — Traded in 1915 to Greenbrier Cheat & Elk for No.1 (1st)
2(1st)	Shay/2-truck-50-ton	1902	180	32	12x12	694	Purchased new by W. Va. Spruce Lbr.
2(2nd)	Shay/3-truck-70-ton	1904	180	32	12x15	836	Purchased new by W. Va. Spruce Lbr.
3	Shay/3-truck-70-ton	1903	180	32	12x15	754	Purchased new by W. Va. Spruce Lbr.
4(1st)	Shay/3-truck-80-ton	1904	200	36	13.5x15	926	Purchased new by W. Va. Spruce Lbr.
4(2nd)	Shay/3-truck-80-ton	1922	200	36	12x15	3189	Birch Valley Lbr. Co. Tioga Lbr. Co. - To Mower in 1943
5	Shay/3-truck-80-ton	1905	200	36	13.5x15	1503	Purchased new by W. Va. Spruce Lbr.
6(1st)	Climax/2-truck-40-ton	1904	180(?)	31(?)	12.5x14(?)	534	WVaP&P No.1 - used 1912/13
6(2nd)	Shay/3-truck-70-ton	1907	200	36	12x15	1907	Lewisburg & Ronceverte RR - to WVaP&P in 1913
7	Shay/2-truck-42-ton	1912	200	29.5	10x12	2563	Purchased new by WVaP&P for constr. of Stoney River Dam at Luke, Md.
8	Shay/3-truck-100-ton	1912	200	40	15x17	2583	Purchased new by WVaP&P
10	Shay/3-truck-70-ton	1914	200	36	12x15	2765	Built for Canadian Gov't. but delivered to WVaP&P
11	Shay/3-truck-100-ton	1914	200	40	15x17	2799	Purchased new by WVaP&P
12	Shay(see Note*)	1921	200	48	17x18	3156	Purchased new by WVaP&P
13	Shay/4-truck-150-ton	1906	200	46	17x18	1586	Chesapeake & Ohio Ry - sold to WVaP&P in 1923
14	Shay/4-truck-150-ton	1910	200	46	17x18	2248	Chesapeake & Ohio Ry - sold to WVaP&P in 1923

*Note - Shay No. 12 was originally built with 3 trucks, weight 154 tons; was rebuilt to 4 trucks and 197(?) tons by Cass shops in 1923.

Dispositions

Number	Subsequent owners/disposition
1(1st)	Traded in 1915 to North Fork Lbr. Co. for 2nd No.1; scrapped by North Fork in 1931
1(2nd)	Cass Scenic RR; then traded to B&O RR Museum (Baltimore) for lease of Western Maryland Ry Shay No. 6
2(1st)	Returned to Lima in 1903 or 1904
2(2nd)	Scrapped in early 1930s at Cass
3	Scrapped in early 1930s
4(1st)	To Conner (or Gilmore) & Tanner Sand & Gravel Co., Columbus, Texas
4(2nd)	In Service on Cass Scenic RR as of this writing
5	In Service on Cass Scenic RR as of this writing
6(1st)	To SI&E as No. 1334; later to Waterford Lbr. Co. as No. 1
6(2nd)	Sold to Preston County Coal Corp. in 1947
7	Sold in 1916/17; various coal company owners; scrapped in early 1950s
8	Scrapped late 1930s
10	To R. E. Wood Lbr. Co. in 1926; Birmingham Rail & Locomotive No. 1698; then The Sound Timber Co. No. 3 in 1928
11	Scrapped late 1930s
12	Retired about 1943; scrapped 1955
13	Retired about 1941; scrapped 1955
14	Sold to Western Maryland Ry in 1932; scrapped in 1953

On this and rosters in following chapters, when conflicting data was found, the information likely to be correct in the opinion of the author is shown on the roster.

Roster by Thomas Lawson, Jr.

Legend
C/N - Construction serial number assigned by the builder at time of construction.
BP - Boiler pressure in working order, expressed in pounds per square inch.
Cylinder size - Diameter of the cylinders and the length of the piston stroke, in inches.

John Krause

In a scene now familiar to tourists and railfans who ride the Cass Scenic Railroad, Mower Lumber Shay No. 4 pauses at the Cass water tank for a drink before heading up the mountain. The tank here is a C&O standard, built by that road to serve both its Greenbrier branch trains (the C&O runs on the other side of the tank), and the lumber road. It once had two penstocks, one on each side to serve both lines.

Phil Ronfor, Ed Crist Coll

(Above) Mower Lumber Shay No. 4 is backing up to the company store at Cass, where it will load provisions on the log flats for the wood hicks encamped up on the mountain. At one time the Cass company store was one of the largest wooden buildings in West Virginia.

Phil Ronfor, Ed Crist Coll.

(Left) In another water tank view at Cass, No. 4 tops off its tank before heading up the mountain in pre-dawn gloom. The Shay will fill up one more time at trackside before reaching Bald Knob.

Mower Lumber Shay No. 4 appears to be jockeying the steam-powered Barnhart log loader into position to tackle the jumble of logs behind it. Is that a man in a suit getting ready to pop a limb into one of the flat car's pole pocket? The date is November 10, 1945.

(both) W. Va. Coll., W. Va. University

A mower Lumber Company logging camp as it appeared in August 1946. The shacks were loaded and moved quickly from place to place. Note the limbs stuffed into the flat cars' pole pockets to hold the logs in place.

Phil Ronfor, Ed Crist Coll.

We're all loaded up and the log train, headed by Mower Lumber Shay No. 1 is about to begin the 26-mile trek back to Cass in October 1956. It will be at least two hours before the train crew can sit down to dinner.

W. Va. Coll., W. Va. University

(Above) Judging by the pile of ties laying around and the hand car trailer, Mower Shay is engaged in some track laying in August 1946.

(Left) An unidentified brakeman couples up a logging flat to Mower Shay No. 4's tank at Cass. Note the lunch bucket on the tank's running board. Not much of a chance of going home for lunch on this job!

Phil Ronfor, Ed Crist Coll.

(Above) As the empty log train moves up the mountain it enters the first of two switchbacks needed to gain vertical distance. Even at this, some of the grades in this area are 11 percent (11 feet of rise to every 100 linear feet). On mainline railroads a two percent grade is considered heavy. The morning fog on this fall day hasn't quite lifted yet.

(Right) Between the first and second switchbacks, No. 4 pushes its train through logged-over grazing land. This area is very familiar to modern-day photographers riding on the scenic railroad's trains, and especially on the railfan specials where photo run-bys are staged in this vicinity.

(Left) Shay No. 1 backs up between the two switchbacks carrying a Western Maryland hopper for interchange with that road at Spruce. This was a rare sight on a Mower log train. The motor car in front of the train is carrying a track crew to do a little maintenance, look for loose bolts and spikes, soft spots, etc.

(Below) On the same October, 1957 day as above, Ronfor photographed No. 1 headed down the original logging road mainline from Old Spruce to Spruce with its WM hopper to hand over to that line. This stretch of track was taken up before the scenic railroad took over. It was recently reinstalled, only to have the WM trackage threatened with abandonment.

In another scene familiar to tourist riders, Shay No. 4 pushes its empty train at the second switchback. Askew number plate on the smokebox door is a matter of little import as far as Mower management was concerned at this late date in its life. The large diamond stacks contained mesh spark arresters, very important on logging railroads, and give the locomotives an older look than they deserve.

Shay No. 4 has just cleared the second switchback on its way to Bald Knob, and is approaching Whittaker station. The gloom of morning fog is no longer evident in this sunny Ronfor photo.

A brisk breeze is blowing No. 4's exhaust as the Shay struggles up Back Allegheny Mountain above the second switchback in November 1956. The fireman has been doing his job as the boiler is popping off.

No. 4 is deep in the "woods" near Whittaker with its train of empties. The valley and mountains in the background are just shedding their shroud of fog in this early November morning in 1956. By the end of the day the train will be making this same trek down the mountain with its load of logs for the mill. Today's tourist line operates in much the same manner, with the locomotive pushing up the mountain and pulling, or braking, down, providing better control of the train on this steep line.

(Left) Nearing its destination at the logging site, No. 4 churns slowly upgrade in dense and isolated woods.

(Below) No. 4's cut of cars rounds a sharp curve with the glory of West Virginia mountain scenery in the background. No wonder this line has become such an attraction since the end of logging!

Coal Smoke and Cheesecake on Bald Knob — A Cass Postscript

On May 25, 1968, the West Virginia Department of Natural Resources officially opened the Cass Scenic Railroad's extension to the top of Bald Knob,* and in honor of the occasion, sent out complimentary tickets to West Virginia politicians, newspersons, and anyone in the national media they thought ought to attend.

Among those receiving the free ducats was the late Freeman Hubbard, longtime editor of *Railroad* Magazine. Since Hubbard was getting along in years at that time and not of a mind to leave the comfort of New York City living for wilds of West Virginia, he sent the tickets to me, and, since I was one of his "stringers" at that time, directed me to bring back a photo essay of the ceremonies and ancillary activities. Since I'd be one of the passengers on the first train to Bald Knob, how could I say no?

Those of you who were regular readers of *Railroad* in the 1960s and 70s will recall Ol' Freeman had a penchant for photographs showing a, um, well-turned ankle. And if you wanted to get your photos between the pages of his magazine, why just include a scantily-clad nubile female in the foreground and your picture was in! No matter if your photograph was of a rotary snowplow battling a Manitoba blizzard or a switching move within a steel mill, just get a young lady, fair of face and form, in the foreground and that was all it took. Today some feminist group would have burned Freeman in effigy for his sexism.

May 25th was a made-to-order Spring day—clear and sunny with just enough breeze to keep things comfortable. And so I boarded the train in Cass, together with West Virginia's Govenor Hulett Smith and the reigning Strawberry Festival Queen, plus assorted brass, various media types, a few local dignitaries, and a gaggle of railfans. With Shays Nos. 4, 7, and 5 pushing for all they were worth we went chugging out of Cass.

When we got to Whittaker Station, were greeted by the Marching Band from nearby Greenbank High School, which was led by half a dozen or so high-stepping majorettes. Well, the majorettes were certainly scantilly-clad by the standards of 1968, and as nubile as all get out. So might as well make the boss happy and photograph these damsels the next time they got up close.

There was speech making before and after the golden spike ceremony, so skipping some of the verbiage I worked my way through the crowd until Governor Smith was right in front of me, properly attired in his dark blue suit and striped engineer's cap. He swung the maul at the spike while the Strawberry Festival Queen peeked over his shoulder.

With the speech making over and the Governor on his way back to the capital, the rest of us were free to amuse ourselves. The weather held and as the Department of Natural Resources ran a couple of trains I chose to hunker down and photograph the Shays. I banged away with the camera and figured that my mentor would get all he could possibly ask for. It was not often that you can have the time of your life while doing a favor for an old man.

Ultimately, I sent the group of photos to Freeman Hubbard and ultimately the pictures of the thundering Shays, of the governor in his engineer's cap and the scantily-clad majorettes appeared in *Railroad* Magazine. Not surprisingly, the governor got a third of a column and the majorettes got half a page.

And that would have been the end of this modest story. However, about a week after the magazine came out, there appeared in my mailbox a letter with an Ohio postmark on it. Inside was a very earnest letter from a youth informing me that the Third Majorette from the Left was the woman of his dreams and could I please send her name, address, and telephone number.

I wrote the lad a gentle letter explaining that, not only did I not have the address and phone number of the Third Majorette from the Left, but I didn't even have her name. I suggested that if he wrote to the Greenbank High School and couched his request in the right terms–do not betray raging hormones–there might be a chance the school would send him the information.

I never did hear from the amorous Buckeye State youth, so to this day I do not know if he was able to contact the Third Majorette from the Left and if so, whether any sort of relationship developed.

Personally, I would have preferred the Second Majorette from the Right.

—William E. Warden

William E. Warden

Greenbank High School band marches at Bald Knob in honor of the opening of the Cass extension May 25, 1968. An Ohio youth fancied the Third Majorette from the Left, but the photographer would have preferred the Second from the Right.

*Reportedly, some unofficial runs were made to Bald Knob at the close of the 1965 operational season.

Cass Scenic Railroad

The state park-operated Cass Scenic Railroad, running on the old Mower logging line has long been one of the best known railroad attractions in the Eastern US and a real boon for tourism in that part of West Virginia.

(Above) It's opening day to Bald Knob on May 25, 1968, and Cass Scenic Railroad Shays Nos. 4, 7, and 5 are pushing a load of dignitaries and just plain train watchers up Back Allegheny Mountain.

(Right) On the same date, in celebration of completion of the tourist operation to the summit, two of the three Shays used that day power a train at Whittaker Station, about half way up the mountain.

(all) William E. Warden

(Left) Early in its career—October 1963 to be exact—Cass Scenic held its first railfan weekend for members of the Old Dominion (Richmond, Va.) and C. P. Huntington (Huntington, W. Va.) National Railway Historical Society Chapters. Shays 4 and 1 doubleheaded a special train through the morning mists from Cass to Whittaker. This is one of the few times that the trains were run engine first. In normal daily operation they push the train up the mountain and back it down.

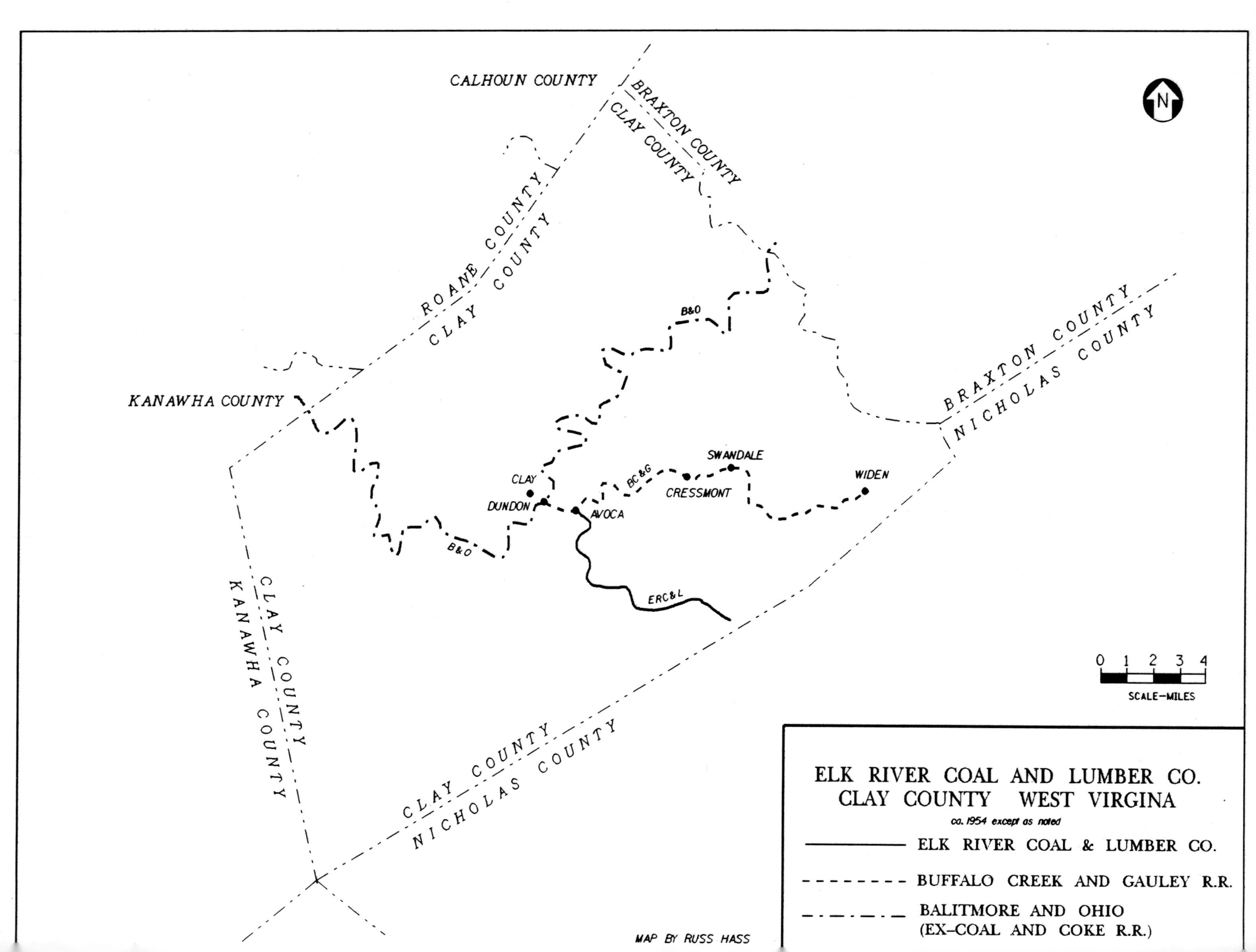

ELK RIVER COAL AND LUMBER CO.
CLAY COUNTY WEST VIRGINIA
ca. 1954 except as noted
ELK RIVER COAL & LUMBER CO.
BUFFALO CREEK AND GAULEY R.R.
BALITMORE AND OHIO
(EX-COAL AND COKE R.R.)
0 1 2 3 4
SCALE–MILES
CALHOUN COUNTY
BRAXTON COUNTY
CLAY COUNTY
ROANE COUNTY
CLAY COUNTY
KANAWHA COUNTY
BRAXTON COUNTY
NICHOLAS COUNTY
CLAY COUNTY
KANAWHA COUNTY
CLAY COUNTY
NICHOLAS COUNTY
B&O
B&O
BC&G
ERC&L
CLAY
DUNDON
AVOCA
CRESSMONT
SWANDALE
WIDEN
MAP BY RUSS HASS

Chapter 4 - Elk River Coal & Lumber Company – W. M. Ritter Lumber Company – Georgia-Pacific (Swandale, Clay County)

If the Greenbrier Cheat & Elk was a corporate boardroom creation, the Elk River Coal & Lumber Company was sired by rugged individualism out of the West Virginia fastness. Those of us who visited the property in the early 1950s onward heard the following story of Elk River Coal & Lumber's origins.

New Jersey native-Joseph G. Bradley was the Elk River's founder and long-time leading figure.

The now-disproven (but often repeated, even in print) story began with Simon Cameron, Abraham Lincoln's Secretary of War. Cameron had been a faithful Republican and trusted Secretary of War and for his trouble, he was awarded a sizeable chunk of West Virginia real estate in 1880—102,000 Clay County acres of virgin timber and coal seams. How the state could own that large a tract of land as late as 1880 and just exactly what Cameron did to merit it was never explained. (A bioghraphical sketch of Cameron in the *Encyclopedia Britannica* says, "He administered the War Department with such favoritism that in January 1862 President Lincoln transferred him to the post of Minister to Russia."—hardly the sort of "services" that would entitle one to over 100,000 acres of land. When Simon died, grandson Joseph Bradley, it was said, inherited the whole tract. Scion of a Boston Brahmin family and Havard educated, Joseph first visited his new empire in 1903 when he was 23.

Young Bradley organized the Elk River Coal and Lumber Company in 1903 and in 1904 the common-carrier Buffalo Creek & Gauley Railroad, beloved of 1960s train watchers was chartered.

This story was, however, discredited by Neva Walling of the Clay County Historical Society, who took the trouble to research deeds and land records of the ERC&L in the County court house. According to her research, The Elk River Coal & Lumber Comapny—originally named The Elk River Coal and Lumber Association—composed of nine Pennsylvania businessmen who purchased 93,000 acres of Clay County land from Henry Murphy and a group of investors representing one W. H. Edwards. One of the nine businessmen was James Cameron, grandson of Simon and *uncle* of Joseph Bradley. The latter, while indeed educated at Harvard, was no Boston Brahmin but was born in New Jersey.

The 93,000 acres were divided into nine tracts of roughly 10,000 acres each, with each of the Pennsylvanians owning one. A down payment was placed on the land, with the rest of the amount to be paid as timber was cut. Squatters and small landholders lived in much of the land and the company's lawyer would make an offer to these people: "Let us take the timber and mineral rights and when we get through timbering the land will be cleared for farming." Most of these individuals accepted the offer but it's questionable whether many lived to see their land cleared, and farming the thin soil on these rocky hillsides was not very profitable.

So it was the Elk River Coal & Lumber Company, not Joseph Bradley, who founded the common-carrier Buffalo Creek & Gauley Railroad. Purists might raise an eyebrow at the "common carrier" label, inasmuch as ERC&L was both the sole owner and the sole freight customer. However, the road did carry passengers, initially in conventional coaches and then in two Mack railbuses, as late as 1959, and did have its own hoppers which were interchanged with foreign lines.

The BC&G eventually ran from coal mines at Widen 18 miles southwestwardly to a connection with the Coal & Coke Railroad--later the Baltimore & Ohio's Charleston-Grafton branch—at Dundon. The C&C had been opened from Charleston to Clay, across the Elk River from Dundon, in January 1897 and it reached Gassaway in September 1904.

About midway on the BC&G main lay the hamlet of Swandale and it was here that the Elk River's rambling lumber mill with its two towering stacks was built. The obligatory millpond was created in a park-like setting just on the other side of the mill in the 1940s; and this is the image of the mill most familiar to railfans who came to Clay County in the 1950s and 1960s.

Four of the nine founders eventually paid off their

Elvin Frame Coll.

The Swandale mill sported only two stacks in this photograph taken about 1920. The third stack, familiar to train watchers in the 1950s and 1960s, was added in the 1940s.

John Krause

This 1950s view of the Swandale mill shows ERC&L Shay No. 12, a 3-truck 80-ton locomotive in its fifth ownership, crude four-wheel bobber caboose, four loaded log flats, and the faithful log loader on the rear. A derelict Climax sits on the left, the mill's activity evident by the steam and smoke around it.

share of the debt on the land and their tracts were partitioned among the remaining five. By 1910 some of the Elk River members had died and left their heirs, including Bradley, a trust administered by a Philadelphia bank which received 5 percent of the amount disbursed as dividends. With that much interest in West Virginia the bank was able to appoint a number of the Elk River board of directors. The heirs were content to let Bradley run things and he eventually became president of the company. However, the board of directors remained Bradle's employer and would become his undoing.

Clay County, or that part of it that was Bradley's empire, was one of the remoter parts of West Virginia. Craggy mountains peppered with miners' and loggers' homes, innocent of paint but not of junked automobiles and refigerators, provided the backdrop. Paved roads were almost non-existent well into the 1950s and were so rudely constructed that one Virginia observer was caused to remark, "West Virginia highways are so narrow that they have only one side to them." (The author has had the experience of finding a Clay County road ending abruptly, even though the state highway map assured him that it would run another 20 miles.)

For this reason, plus his attention being foused on coal mining, may account for the fact that Bardley did not begin developing his timber holdings along the Lilly Fork until 1916 (or 1910 depending on which source you use), making him a late-comer to the logging industry. It should be noted that Bradley was not the first logger in Clay County. C. L. Ritter Lumber Company, for example, had operated a mill at Avoca, between Cressmont and Dundon, around the turn of the century and employed two 42-inch gauge, 17-ton Climaxes. In addition, Crescent Lumber Company operated a mill at Cressmont, at the site of what later became the BC&G's Cressmont Dairy; it too relied on a narrow-gauge Climax. Crescent appears to have cut timber along the Hickory Fork and Wallowhole Fork, both of which flow into Buffalo Creek near Cressmont.

The Lilly Fork was several miles removed from Swandale and the logging railroad joined the BC&G tracks at Avoca, about a mile east of Dundon, where there was a wye for turning the engines. Thus we had the daily spectacle of little Shay- and Climax-powered logging trains rubbing elbows (cylinders maybe) with 50-car coal trains on the common carrier BC&G. No problem getting trackage rights since log cuts and coal drags all ran at the behest of Bradley. In fact, the logging engines could frequently be seen powering work trains on the BC&G. Dressed lumber rode aboard ERC&L flats and B&O box cars cut into regular BC&G trains.

Bradley's land was rich in oak, beech, hickory, the ubiquitous chestnut, and poplar. One poplar is reported to have been 88 feet to the first limb. To get this timber out of the woods, he purchased new Climaxes E-1 and E-2 in 1916 and 1918, respectively, to wander up the Lilly Fork—and sometimes through that stream with a

A. A. Thieme

Somewhere along the Lilly Fork, amid the hardwoods of Clay County, Climax No. E-3 waits patiently in the late 1950s. The men barely visible to the right are replacing crudely hewn ties (seen both in the track under the engine and stracked on the flat car).

carefree air that would have been undignified for a rod engine—for 15 miles (down to 8-10 miles when the logging operation was discontinued) in pursuit of logs.

A third Climax—the last Climax ever built, by some accounts—numbered E-3 came on line in 1928, while a fourth was around briefly in the 1940s. By the time this author turned up on the property for the first time, only E-3 had escaped the scrapper's torch and it lay forlornly in a clutter of wheels, tires, and other impedimentia at Swandale. But even the most forlorn steamer can be brought back to life, more or less, and today E-3 is on display at California's Roaring Camp & Big Trees Narrow Gauge Railroad (a tourist line).

How to explain Bradley's dogged devotion to a locomotive type so seldom favored by loggers? Perhaps a man of Bradley's will and determination would be hard put to admit a mistake. After all, this was the man who had stared down the United Mine Workers Union and survived a particularly bloody strike in 1952-3 that saw a BC&G passenger train held up at gun point and one of the railroad's bridges dynamited. Perhaps there was sentimental attachment; this was the man who organized company picnics, guaranteed the children of employees jobs upon graduation from high school and paid his non-unionized people substantially more than union wages (but wrote scolding letters to tenants who failed to keep the lawns of his company houses neat). Possibly it was just that the Climaxes were ideally suited for the Elk River Coal & Lumber Company's logging operation.

Perhaps the Climax fetish was an abberation, for around 1950 Bradley acquired former Lackawanna Lumber Co. Shay No. 10 to work the Lilly Fork as ERC&L No. 12. Then in 1957 he purchased two Shays, nearby Cherry River Boom & Lumber Company's Nos. 2 and 7. (The author found No. 2, still wearing its huge CRB&L number, in July of that year.) No. 7, alas, was never put in use at Dundon and was cut up for spare parts in 1959.

It used to be said of one Caribbean island that the residents made a living taking in each other's washing. Something similar could be said about West Virginia loggers and shortlines because they were forever buying each other's surplus locomotives. In this case the seller was Cherry River Boom & Lumber company, about which we shall learn more on succeeding pages. One of the two second-hand Shays which became ERC&L No. 19, is believed to have been the last steam locomotive in day-to-day logging service east of the Mississippi. (Ely-Thomas Shay No. 2 was actually in use after No. 19 was retired, but only for yard switching.) That No. 19 should have that honor says much about the staying power of both Shay and Elk River's logging operation.

By West Virginia standards, Elk River was a small operation. Total trackage from Avoca up Lilly Fork was on the order of 10 miles by the 1950s and a year's mill output averaged 5,000,000 board feet. A single daily five-car-and-caboose train under the command of engineer Creed Truman and conductor Brooks Litton was the norm. When track was being relaid, a steel train consisting of one of the geared engines and one or two flats cars of rail and ties would occasionally wander up Lilly Fork too.

Trains left Swandale in the late 1950s around 6:30 a.m., after conductor Litton received trackage rights over BC&G from Swandale to Avoca. This timing would usually get the log train to the Avoca wye before a BC&G train of eastbound empties got to that point. If the log train was late, usually there would be a meet around Cressmont with the log train taking the siding. Depending on how much work it had to do, the log train would arrive back at Swandale between 3 and 5 p.m.

Fords on the Lilly Fork were almost as numerous as crossties—well maybe that's an exaggeration; however, they were the source of several tales. Standard practice in fording a stream seems to have been to shut off the throttle as the stream was approached, coast through the water, and then crack the throttle as the other creek bank was reached. By the time the throttle was opened, the locomotive would be pointed upgrade and trying to accelerate on wet rails. Frequently this resulted in what was a rare spectacle—a Shay actually loosing its footing, to the delight of any nearby train wtacher.

John Krause

ERC&L Climax No. 3 seems to be enjoying its favorite passtime—fording the Lilly Fork. Flat car provides accommodations for a logging crew headed someplace upstream.

If the water in the creek was particularly high, a flat car was pushed through the ford ahead of the locomotive. If the car stayed on the track the train could proceed! Occasionally, water would slosh into the firebox and to all external appearances, the fire would be out. However, the coals were so hot beneath the surface that the fuel would usually reignite itself.

The fords did have one virtue, however: when one of the Shays became thirsty, it was a trifing matter to drop a hose into a nearby ford and siphon up enough water to top off the locomotive's tank. Additionally, fords did not wash away in floods as did bridges and cost little to build.

Swandale itself boasted a population of barely 200 people in 1950. Most of them resided in company houses that Joseph Bradley had caused to be erected on a hillside overlooking the mill. Like Cass, Swandale was a company town, complete with a company store, a community center, a miniscule post office, and a baseball field. Probably because it came into existence much later and loggers were mostly family men living in their own homes, Swandale was never the raucous community that Cass was. A horse-drawn wagon was sill making home deliveries from the local store well into the 1950s, and Bradley was providing all the company houses with coal from his Rich Run Mine at Widen.

Some writers have suggested that the coal miner's bloody strike in the early 1950s took more out of Bradley than he was willing to admit, and that it was his physical condition that led to the eventual break up of his Clay County empire. This is conjecture, of course, but the author is inclined to give it credence.

However, ERC&L had run up some $3 million in debt by the mid-1950s and its pension fund was in jeopardy. It was the Philadelphia bank whose members sat on the company's board that finally sold it and the BC&G for $5 million in 1958 to Clinchfield Coal Company, a division of The Pittston Company (which itself was involved in a prolonged miners' strike in 1989-90).

Bradley, as his Uncle Jim's executor, was involved in some business with Cameron's estate in Pennsylvania when the sale went through and was not even consulted on the matter. As historian Walling put it, "He [Bradley] did not sell out. He was evicted before he knew it. He simply sent for his belongings and had the rest burned." Having his empire sold out from under him probably accounts for Bradley's bitterness and refusal to discuss anything about Clay County in his later years when this writer tried to interview him.

"Coal" in the corporate title connotes little interest in lumber or any other commodities and Pittston very quickly sold off 50,000 acres of remaining timber land along the Lilly Fork, plus the Swandale mill and the logging railroad to Columbus, Ohio-based W. M. Ritter Lumber Company. At the same time, Pittston shut down the company store at Widen and the company dairy at Cressmont, midway between Dundon and Swandale. (ERC&L had been as nearly self-sufficient as a coal and lumber company could be.) Ritter itself was subsequently merged into Georgia-Pacific Corporation on January 1, 1961.

The Widen coal mine was shut down on December 30, 1963, its coal seam ostensibly played out, and it appeared that the logging operation and railroad might shut down too, for with the mine no longer operating, the BC&G's only traffic was a thrice-weekly lumber train from Swandale to the B&O interchange at Dundon. Shay No. 19, its smokebox now decked out in imitation aluminum, was put up for sale and replaced by Georgia-Pacific's own locomotive, a 44-ton Plymouth diesel.

With no coal to haul, Clinchfield sought and received permission to abandon the Buffalo Creek & Gauley. The last BC&G train between Swandale and Dundon ran on February 27, 1965. Thereafter, the Plymouth diesel took over the job of hauling finished lumber to Dundon. But Georgia-Pacific saw the supply of merchantable timber dwindling and the cost of logging what remained growing constantly. In 1968, the logging operation in Clay County was terminated. By this time trucks were hauling the lumber to Dundon for loading on flat cars at the B&O interchange.

Today Swandale is a virtual ghost town and weeds and trees cover the remains of the company store's crumbling foundation. Hardly any traces remain of the Swandale mill.

With the cessation of logging, Clay County lost its only industry of any magnitude and loggers joined coal miners and railroaders in the ranks of the unemployed. But don't fault Georgia-Pacific management entirely. Most corporate officials had never operated log loaders and probably few had ever seen the inside of a double-band sawmill. But they were familiar with the bottom line on a balance sheet. And they were acutely aware that if that bottom line had a minus sign in front of it too often irate stockholders would soon replace them with more practical people.

Still, one cannot help but speculate that if Joseph Bradley's health had not failed him or if he had been in Clay County at the time of the sale to Pittston and had stayed at the helm of ERC&L, perhaps, just perhaps, the smokey stemwinders might have continued hauling logs down the Lilly Fork for a few more years.

C. W. Jernstrom, W. E. Warden Coll.

ERC&L Shay No. 19, one car of logs and a loader near Swandale in September 1958.

Elvin Frame

(Above) Overhead view of the Swandale Elk River Coal & Lumber Co. Mill about 1940. Why some of the finished timbers are stacked very neatly and others in a haphazard jumble we don't know. Some of what appear to be railroad crosstie-size timbers have been loaded on a flatcar. The mill shows its age with discolored siding. ***(Below)*** Shay No. 12 has brought a train of logs to the mill in this 1950s photo (note the mill has been painted!) A part of the mill pond is visible to the right. Also to the right of the train is a coal hopper and a conveyor belt for unloading.

John Krause

Locomotives of Elk River Coal & Lumber Co. — W. M. Ritter Lumber Co. — Georgia-Pacific							
No.	Type	Date Built	BP (psi)	Driver size	Cylinder size/stroke	C/N	Previous Owners
12	Shay/3-truck-80-ton	1902	180	36	14.5x12	687	Lackawanna Lbr. Co. (No. 10) Emporium Lbr. Co. (No. 10) Emporium Forestry (No.40) Heywood-Wakefield (No. 40)
18	Shay/3-truck-65-ton	1904	180	36	12x15	916	Cherry River Boom & Lbr. Co. (No. 7)
19	Shay/3-truck-65-ton	1905	180	36	12x15	1568	Tioga Lbr. Co. (No. 2) Birch Valley Lbr. Co. (No. 2) Cherry River Boom & Lbr. Co. (No. 2[3rd])
20	Plymouth Diesel-44-ton	?	NA	?	NA	?	
E-1	Climax-30-ton	1916	?	?	11x12	1413	Purchased new by ERC&L
E-2	Climax-45-ton	1918	200	33	12.5x14	1501	Purchased new by ERC&L
E-3	Climax-50-ton	1928	200	33	12.5x14	1692	Purchased new by ERC&L
E-4	Climax-70-ton	1920	200	35	14.5x16	1579	Spice Run Lbr. Co. (No. 5) Dawkins Lbr. Co.

Dispositions

Number	Subsequent owners/disposition
12	Scrapped 1962
18	Dismantled for spare parts 1959; never used or renumbered to ERC&L
19	Sold to Dry Gulch Jct. & Tombstone RR in Wytheville, Va. (tourist line), now at Lima, Ohio, for display at Allen County Historical Society.
20	Scrapped 1975
E-1	Scrapped about 1930
E-2	Scrapped about 1962
E-3	Sold to Carroll Park & Western tourist RR; now under restoration by Roaring Camp & Big Trees Railroad (tourist line) in California; converted to 36-inch gauge by RC&BT; was 48-inch gauge at CP&W.
E-4	Scrapped before 1950

Roster by Thomas Lawson, Jr.

Legend
C/N - Contruction serial number assigned by builder at time of construction.
BP - Boiler pressure in working order, expressed in pounds per square inch.
Cylinder size/stroke - diameter of the cylinders and the length of the piston stroke, in inches.

W. M. Ritter's Swandale Yard was nothing if not cluttered. It is a raw gray March 1960 day and Shay No. 12 has been out of service for some time. Poking out of the engine house at left is Climax No. 3. At right, still wearing the Elk River Coal & Lumber Company logo, is the tank of Climax No. 2.

William E. Warden

John Krause

ERC&L Shay No. 12 is running somewhere on the BC&G mainline between Dundon and Swandale on a crisp November day in 1956. No. 12 was originally built for the Lackawanna Lumber Company in 1902, and after passing through four owners, came to Elk River Coal & Lumber. It was ultimately scrapped in 1962.

William E. Warden

Proof—if any were needed—that a Shay can go anywhere is this photo of ERC&L No. 19 (ex-Cherry River Boom & Lumber No. 2) casually fording the Lilly Fork. Why waste money on a bridge that would have to be relocated in a year or two anyhow? The Shay doesn't mind. Like No. 12, No. 19 had several previous owners (two before Cherry River Boom & Lumber), having been built in 1905. It was a 65-ton locomotive.

Howard W. Ameling

Sometime before the end of its days in West Virginia and before being shipped to the Carroll Park & Western tourist railroad, Climax No. 3 was restored to operating condition and given a coat of aluminum paint on its stack and smokebox (photographed at Dundon, June 5, 1962). No. 3 is now at the Roaring Camp and Big Trees narrow gauge tourist line in Felton, California.

J. Madden

(Left) A spot familiar to train watchers in the early 1960s was Dundon, home of the Buffalo Creek & Gauley. A cut of cars in the center includes lumber from Elk River Coal & Lumber's Swandale mill. The curving track to the right is the B&O line to Charleston, and at left is a sagging log loader and some Elk River logging flats that apparently have been doing track work. Elk River company houses can be seen in the background.

John Krause

Will the crew of men aboard the flat–probably track men judging by the spike keg and other tools aboard–get splashed as Elk River Coal & Lumber Climax No. 3 plunges across the Lilly Fork? Possibly, but the photographer gives no clue.

Elk River's Shay No. 12 and Barnhart log loader are diligently at work in the forestland along the Lilly Fork. No. 12 shows signs of rebuilding sometime in its checkered past as evidenced by the oddly shaped cab window and the uneven coal bunker and water trunk.

After taking siding for a Buffalo Creek & Gauley freight, Elk River Coal & Lumber Shay No. 12 prepares to back onto the BC&G main at Cressmont. Building at right is the former Cressmont Dairy, which was part of logging and coal baron Joseph Bradley's empire. At one time Crescent Lumber Company had a mill at Cressmont (hence the name), but it was only a faded memory when this photo was taken.

all (John Krause)

Look hard and you'll see a complete ERC&L logging train picking up logs, bobber caboose, a half-loaded flat, the log loader riding atop the cars, and five more cars for loading, with a Shay for power.

John Krause

This impressive "in-the-woods" photo of Elk River's Climax No. 3 shows its crew awaiting instructions from the track gang working behind it. The track seems to be actually laid in a live stream bed! Logs in the background have been skidded to this locality for pick-up. Fifty-ton No. 3 was one of four Climaxes owned by ERC&L, having been bought new in 1928. If not the very last Climax locomotive ever built, No. 3 was certainly one of the last.

Phil Ronfor, Ed Crist Coll.

Again, track laying is the work as Climax No. 2 carries two flats loaded with rough-hewn ties and tools. There is no roadway beyond where the men are working so this represents construction to a new part of the woods for fresh logging operations. No. 2 was a 45-ton locomotive purchased new by Elk River in 1918.

Shay No. 12 nonchalantly wades through the Lilly Fork in the summer of 1960, with a train load of logs. Steam locomotives could easily ford streams of low depth, just as long as the water didn't reach the ashpan of the firebox, usually well above the rails. Diesels have great difficulty in water since their electric traction motors are slung low around the axles of the driving wheels.

William E. Warden

(both) John Krause

(Left) Here Elk River Coal & Lumber's Shay No. 12 is working on BC&G's 1957 track rehabilitation program, dumping off crossties from a C&O gondola. Over 15,000 new ties were placed during this rehabilitation. It's not often that a geared logging locomotive is seen crossing so substantial and permanent a bridge structure. No. 12 was more at home on spindly cribbed trestles or fording the creeks.

(Below) No. 12 is in more familiar territory and doing more usual work as it hauls five loads of logs slowly toward Swandale in the late afternoon sun, spreading a cloud of acrid coal smoke over the forest. This load represents an average day's work at the time this photo was taken in the mid-1950s

This excellent overhead view of Climax No. 3 working in front of a bobtailed "steel train," a sign that once again ERC&L is either picking up or or laying down new track (or maybe both). Engineer Raymond Davis is leaning out of the cab window to check on things. The flat car has kegs of spikes, a tool box, a valise, and a great jumble of track tools, including tongs, lining bars, and jacks–all indispensable in laying rail–as well as a single "stick" of light rail.

(all John Krause)

(Above) What is the crewman of ERC&L's four-wheel caboose thinking as he takes his leisure on the rear platform of the car as the loaded log train chuffs slowly toward Swandale. Probably home, a hot meal and a bath. Its been a long day in the woods. Shay No. 12 is on the point.

(Right) Life in the slow lane! Elk River Shay No. 19 and the log train crew wait near Avoca wye for a westbound BC&G coal train to clear the main line. Once the coal train is past, No. 19 and its load of logs will chug leisurely to Swandale.

W. M. Ritter Operations

John Krause

Shay No. 19, now lettered for Ritter Lumber, smokes past the Swandale mill with another load of logs for the millpond, past stacks of finished lumber ready for shipment via the BC&G and B&O to points far and near.

(Left) Its cylinder, gears, and wheels brightly lit in the late afternoon September sun, W. M. Ritter Shay No. 19 is returning to Swandale Lumber Mill afther a hard day in the woods up the Lilly Fork. The Ritter name is plainly lettered over a painted-out ERC&L logo on the water tank side.

(Right) Shay No. 19 blows off steam whle parked beside the Swandale millpond, filled with logs ready to go to the mill. This photo is a good and very artistic statement about lumber railroading, with the Shay simmering, partially hidden by foliage, and the cut logs in the foreground, all in leafy surroundings.

John Killoran

(Above) Snowstorms don't stop logging operations nor railroad photographers. Shay No. 19, now owned, along with the mill, railroad, and land, by Georgia-Pacific, but still lettered for Ritter, bucks the December 1960 weather near Swandale.

Elmer Treolar, W. E. Warden Coll.

(Left) No. 19 whips around a curve with another load of "Paul Bunyon's toothpicks," bound for the Swandale mill. Judging from the relaxed posture of the brakeman sitting cross-legged on the pilot beam, the Shay is probably not doing more than 15 mph, but for a Shay that's going flat out!

William E. Warden

This shaggy-looking four-wheel bobber caboose is still in use by Georgia-Pacific as the flatcars of logs that flank it attest. We are at the Swandale mill in September 1962. These crews were lucky–most logging trains did not have such an accomodation.

Memorial Day 1960 found W. M. Ritter Shay No. 19 teamed with Buffalo Creek & Gauley 2-8-0 No. 4. The two locomotives are pulling a BC&G excursion train from Dundon to Widen and are now just west of Swandale. The autos pacing the train are a foretaste of what would soon become a common practice as steam excursions began to proliferate.

John Krause

(Right) No. 19 is again seen as the afternoon sun is sinking. The four-car log train is on the BC&G headed toward Swandale in September 1959. This is about the normal length of a W. M. Ritter log train in those days.

David G. Knox

(Below) Someone's hung a "for sale" sign under the headlight of Georgia-Pacific's No. 19 at Swandale in the summer of 1965. The reason for the sign is quite evident: G-P Plymouth diesel No. 20 at left has taken over the log and finished lumber hauling now that the BC&G has folded.

John Krause

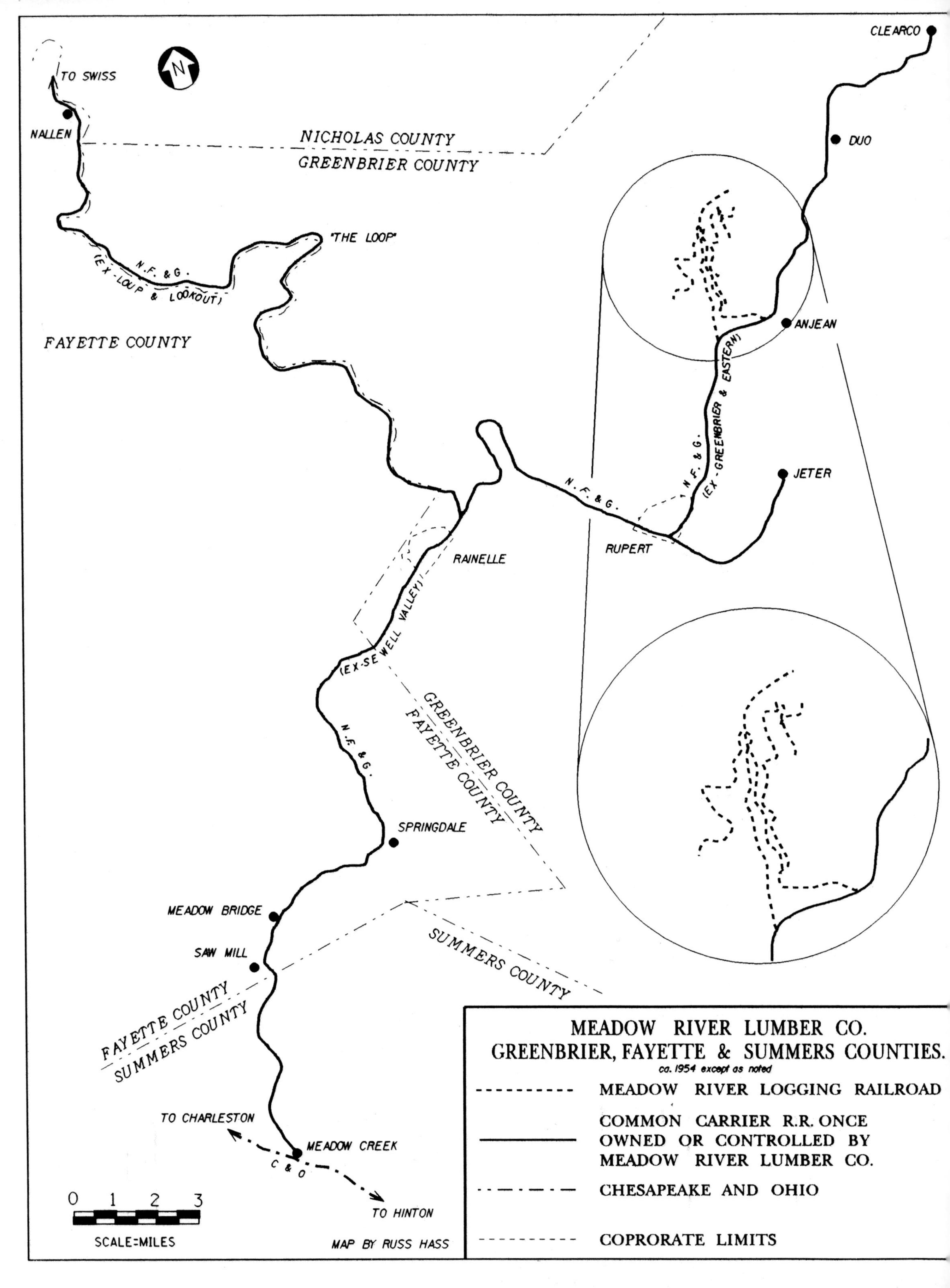
TO SWISS
N
NALLEN
NICHOLAS COUNTY
GREENBRIER COUNTY
CLEARCO
DUO
"THE LOOP"
N.F. & G.
(EX-LOUP & LOOKOUT)
FAYETTE COUNTY
ANJEAN
N.F. & G.
(EX-GREENBRIER & EASTERN)
JETER
N.F. & G.
RUPERT
RAINELLE
(EX-SEWELL VALLEY)
N.F. & G.
GREENBRIER COUNTY
FAYETTE COUNTY
SPRINGDALE
MEADOW BRIDGE
SAW MILL
SUMMERS COUNTY
FAYETTE COUNTY
SUMMERS COUNTY
TO CHARLESTON
MEADOW CREEK
C & O
TO HINTON
0 1 2 3
SCALE=MILES
MAP BY RUSS HASS
MEADOW RIVER LUMBER CO.
GREENBRIER, FAYETTE & SUMMERS COUNTIES.
ca. 1954 except as noted
MEADOW RIVER LOGGING RAILROAD
COMMON CARRIER R.R. ONCE OWNED OR CONTROLLED BY MEADOW RIVER LUMBER CO.
CHESAPEAKE AND OHIO
COPRORATE LIMITS

Chapter 5 — Meadow River Lumber Company (Rainelle, Greenbrier County)

If ever there were a logging railroad made to order for trainwatchers, it was Meadow River Lumber Company's.

The lower end of the line was right on the south side of US Route 60, the main highway from Virginia to Charleston before Interstate 64 drained off the through traffic, and a Charleston-bound traveler need only slow down to see a Shay and Heisler going about their work near the huge sawmill. On the east side of the state road to Hinton, within sight of the mill at Rainelle, were the yards of the Nicholas, Fayette & Greenbrier Railroad, jointly owned by the New York Central and the Chesapeake & Ohio (now Conrail and CSXT). An unwary traveler checking into Rainelle's Pioneer Hotel, hard by the NF&G and Meadow River Yards could plan on being awakened by the nocturnal switching operatons going on below.

Creation of the Meadow River Lumber Company can be credited to two Ohio brothers, lumbermen John and Thomas W. Raine, after whom the town of Rainelle was named.

Like Elk River Coal & Lumber's Joseph Bradley, the Raine brothers were both stern and paternalistic. They built the town's first school, and company houses were equipped early on with running water, toilets, and electricity, and rented for as little as $6.50 per month when new. Thomas Raine also arranged for fresh fruit from Florida to be shipped in to Rainelle's children during the winter. All hands at a logging camp that went three months without an accident received turkey dinners too. Small wonder that the men were affectionately known as "Uncle Johnny" and "Uncle Tommy." In fact, so liked were the Raine brothers that in 1928, Uncle Johnny was elected to the West Virginia House of Delegates, making him the first Republican from Greenbrier County to be elected in 50 years!

This largesse even extended to accomodations for wood hicks. By 1930 a logging camp train was employed as a substitute for the traditional fetid stationary logging camp. (It wasn't until the mid-1940s that Mower Lumber replaced its stationary camps with camp trains.) One car of the train was used for food storage. Next to it was a kitchen car, followed by the dining car. A washroom and lounge, plus several cars fitted out with steel beds completed the train.

Not exactly high-class accommodations, but it did provided a degree of comfort unknown in other logging camps. Then too, the camp could always be hauled right up to the spot where logging was going on, thus eliminating the need for the men to make a long commute to work every day. The one area in which the Raines were not generous was pay. In the 1950s Meadow River wages for millhands were among the lowest in the state and that fact was eventually the company's undoing.

Although the Meadow River timber lands were not as extensive as some operations we've reviewed, they were still large–75,000 acres in 1929 at the peak of the lumber production. Or, to look at it another way, more than 117 square miles. The land area of New York's largest borough, Queens, by comparison, is 113 square miles. By 1952, Meadow River's land totaled 125,000 acres, about the size of Queens plus Brooklyn.

In 1901 John Raine joined the C. E. Andrews Lumber Company of Pennsylvania to form the Raine-Andrews Lumber Company on Gladys Fork of the Cheat River. Raine-Andrews was profitable but the brothers were not satisfied with having just one company. Brother John located some property on Laurel Creek in 1904–possibly the same land that Ely-Thomas later logged (see page 87)—that seemed suitable to their needs and brother Tom told him to buy it. John was at that time busy arranging bark peeling contracts and before he could examine the land, the option to buy it that the brothers had taken out on this property expired and the price

Baldwin Loco. Works, T. W. Dixon Coll.

Sewell Valley 2-8-2 No. 6 was built by Baldwin in 1919. It came to the C&O in the NF&G creation, but was soon sold. Sewell Valley's power, like that of the BC&G, was separate and distinct from the lumber company, though both were owned by the same interests.

T. W. Dixon Coll.

This 1910 photo shows Sewell Valley Shay No. 1, built that year, with the line's ancient ex-Pennsylvania Railroad wooden combine ready to make its daily round trip to Meadow Creek and connection with C&O local trains Nos. 13 and 14 around 1:00 p.m. Later Sewell Valley purchased some gasoline motor cars for its passenger service and rod locomoitives for its freights, and divorced itself from use of logging locomotives.

was raised $10 an acre. The brothers lost interest and subsequently purchased 32,000 acres of largely virgin hardwood from the heirs of Joseph L. Beury, an early coal operator in the New River Valley in Summers County. The Raines' took title to the land for $30 per acre in 1906 and four years later, on September 10, 1910, the mill at Rainelle sawed its first log.

Meadow River's holdings were at some distance from Rainelle, through a largely unchartered and inaccessible countryside of chestnut, oak, maple, birch, and poplar-covered mountains, some rising above 4,000 feet in elevation. (Meadow River's logo, adopted in the late 1920s and still in use in the early 1960s, included a triangle with one of these words "Chestnut," "Poplar," and "Oak," in each of its sides. Where in the late 1920s and later the company was getting chestnut we do not know.) To reach these lands, Thomas Raine, leaving Raine-Andrews in charge of brother John, built a common-carrier line, the Sewell Valley Railroad, to connect the properties with the C&O at Meadow Creek below Hinton on the New River and the mill at Rainelle on the north, finally ending at Rainelle Junction, just north of the town.

Construction started in 1907 and by 1912, the Sewell Valley could boast of 21 miles of track (two miles more than that of the Buffalo Creek & Gauley), and four switchbacks (eliminated in 1949) to allow the track to climb 1,600 feet from the New River Valley at Meadow Creek and then drop 400 feet into Rainelle. The railroad had a short branchline of its own, which ran through the poetically-named hamlet of Spring Dale (Springdale on older maps) and a community called simply "Saw Mill."

Two spanking new Shays were on Meadow River Lumber property by the time the Sewell Valley was completed. Lima delivered two-truck No. 1 (which eventually ended up at Steamtown in Scranton, Pennsylvania) in 1910 and three-truck No. 2 in 1911. Shay No. 3, also new and with three trucks, was added to the stable in 1913. And Sewell Valley possessed in its own right two-truck Shay No. 1, later Meadow River Lumber No. 4.

Tom Raine may have fancied himself the James J. Hill of logging railroads, for in the same year he began the Sewell Valley, he also chartered the Loop & Lookout Railroad Company to run tracks northwest from Rainelle Junction 20 miles to the town of Nallen in Fayette County. Construction was slow at first and by 1912 the Loop & Lookout could boast but five miles of track. However, the rails did reach Nallen in 1916, and in 1930, when the route was Nicholas, Fayette & Greenbrier property, track was laid eastward from Swiss, already on the NYC, an additional 28 miles through Carnifex Ferry to Nallen. Nallen also became the site of the Wilderness Lumber Company's band mill. This company logged chestnut, maple, oak, poplar, hickory, and even basswood in Fayette County, and operated a Shay-powered narrow gauge railroad.

Although the name "Loop & Lookout" sounds, well, quaint, consider that the track wound around a finger of Fayette County that jutted into the Meadow River Valley and was commonly known as "The Loop," and, further, that the town of Lookout is just southwest of Nallen. So the rail line's name does make good sense.

Since the Loop & Lookout had no connection with the outer world except for the Sewell Valley and its connection with the C&O, it should come as no surprise that the SV leased the Loop & Lookout, with the lumber company owning the former.

T. W. Dixon Coll.

Meadow River Lumber Shay No. 1 at more familiar work, bringing a log train onto the Sewell Valley main line in 1918.

Still a third common carrier, the Greenbrier & Eastern, was chartered that same year by a group of coal mine operators to tap seams around Marfrance and Quinwood, albeit not completed until 1921, and run out of Rupert, where it connected with a seven-mile branch of the Sewell Valley from Rainelle Junction. According to a contemporary issue of *Railway and Locomotive Engineering,* the G&E's first locomotive, a superheated Baldwin 2-8-2 with 45,750 pounds tractive effort, was "...designed for operation on curves of 25 degrees and grades as steep as 5.3 per cent," appropriate figures for a logging railroad although its stated purpose was hauling coal.

The railroad followed the Meadow River southeast to Greenbrier & Eastern Junction near Rupert, then wandered northward through the mountains of Greenbrier County, past Anjean, to Clearco, some 20 miles from Rainelle. A branch ultimately ran from Rupert to Jeter.

T. W. Dixon Coll.

G&E added this snappy light Baldwin 2-8-2 to its roster in 1923, duplicate to its No. 1 in size and power. It became C&O No. 2931 after the NF&G merger, and was sold almost immedaitely to Campbell's Creek Railroad, another West Virginia shortline.

Anjean, by the way, is a name calculated to stir the memory of some of our older readers as it was a favorite spot for train watchers and logging aficianados to hunker down on scenic mountainsides of the Gauley Coal & Land Company (Meadow River had timber rights there) and watch logs being skidded and loaded onto the logging trains from grandstand seats, as it were.

Meadow River Lumber had trackage rights on all three shortlines and, save for logging spurs–the longest of which was 20 miles–off these roads and the Rainelle Yard tracks, it had no tracks of its own. Hence, when we speak of Meadow River Lumber's logging railroad we are talking of the confederation of the three shortlines radiating out of Rainelle. They all were sold to the Chesapeake & Ohio on July 1, 1927, forming the C&O's Sewell Valley Branch, and then consolidated into the Nicholas, Fayette & Greenbrier Railroad in 1931. Sewell Valley locomotives were simply added to the C&O motive power roster, but sold off soon thereafter as too small to be useful to the big road. (Don't look for the NF&G in your *Official Guide*; both the C&O and NYC maintained separate listings and a look at the *Guide's* index shows both roads in Meadow Creek, Rainelle, Nallen, and Clearco.) Tom Raine's son, James "Mont" Raine, was made the NF&G's assistant superintendent.

By the time the Meadow River rail empire reached its apex it could claim 142 miles of track. On these rails ran 18 rod and geared locomotives. Passenger service on the Sewell Valley—in the beginning sometimes limited to a box or flat car tucked into a regular logging train but subsequently in the form of a fine wooden open-platform ex-Pennsylvania Railroad combine car hauled by SV No. 1 or 4—was started early on with connections to C&O local train Nos. 13 and 14 at Meadow Creek. The combine car was retired in 1921 and service was provided by Brill motor cars thererafter.

Ultimately, the rail cars provided passenger service out of Rainelle to Nallen and Clearco as well as Meadow Creek. This service was continued by the NF&G after it took over operation of the Sewell Valley Branch. If you wanted to check out trains to these places in your *Official Guide* you looked under Chesapeake & Ohio. However, the NYC seems to have disclaimed all interest in the passenger operation. The passenger trains were finally discontinued in 1948, another victim of the horseless carriage, US Route 60, and a passable road from Rainelle to Hinton.

It is hard to run a West Virginia shortline railroad very far without hitting a coal seam, particularly when you've built it on land once owned by a coal operator, and the Sewell Valley was no exception. But with the railroad owned by a logging company primarily for its own convenience, coal operators had no say in the matter of what the Raines' chose to charge them for haulage.

After considerable yammering by the mine owners about losing out to the competition because of transportation costs, the Interstate Commerce Commission forced Meadow River to sell off the Sewell Valley and the Loop & Lookout in 1921. But not to worry: the new owner was the same Tom Raine.

If it wasn't the biggest in area, Meadow River could

T. W. Dixon Coll.

Sewell Valley used motor cars for employee transportation and also for carrying passengers and mail on occasion. Here operator Chink Fleshman has several passengers on his mail run from the C&O connection at Meadow Creek.

William E. Warden

On a bitterly cold day in 1959, Heisler No. 6 shifts in the Rainelle Yard. C&O cabooses in background are on the adjoining NF&G, jointly owned by NYC and C&O after its creation from the SV, G&E and some new construction in the early 1930s.

claim to have the largest-volume hardwood manufacturing plant in the world. The author has seen somewhat conflicting figures for output of this tripple-band mill—the only one in the state—varying from 110,000 board feet per day average for a ten-hour shift, to 31,644,200 feet cut in the peak year of 1928, to "300,000 feet of lumber per day," quoted in the *Semi-Centennial History of West Virginia*, where a "day" consisted of two 10-hour shifts. If we accept the 1928 figure as being reliable, Meadow River, at the peak of production, shipped on the order of 32 carloads per week of finished hardwood.

In its halcyon days the mill supplied parquet flooring for New York's Waldorf-Astoria Hotel ballroom, caskets, patterns for British submarine chasers, and until 1958, was the world's largest producer of women's shoe heels. And Henry Ford admired Meadow River products as a source of wooden spokes for the wheels of his Model T's and A's.

Eleven lumber docks, each 1,300 feet long, lined the Rainelle Yard and lumber was stacked almost 40 feet high on each dock. Meadow River even built its own 40-foot skeleton flat cars. (Unlike common carrier flat cars, built up from girders, Meadow River's scratch-built log cars were simply wooden platforms held together with truss rods and set atop archbar trucks, although the company later built steel skeleton cars riding on Andrews trucks).

No matter how you slice it, the Rainelle mill was major league. During the 1950s and 1960s trains of empties, sometimes running as many as 20 (a long train by logging standards) would leave Rainelle late in the afternoon. Twelve or 14 loads would come back from the woods long after dark, with the remaining empty cars being used as spacers for the accommodation of tree-length logs, a practice begun in 1939, reputedly an industry first.

At first glance, this timetable seems a tad strange. Loading logs after dark was impractical. However, the trains simply exchanged their empties for cars that had been loaded during daylight. Since the logging crews were living in their portable bunkhouses right at the site of the logging operation, they could start loading last night's delivery of empties early in the morning and not lose time waiting for them to arrive from Rainelle. A geared locomotive, usually either Shay No. 3 or 5, would remain on site at all times to jockey the cars for loading, and Heisler No. 6 usually farried loads and empties between Rainelle and the logging site. Shay No. 5 had the honor of being one of the few Shays rebuilt with piston valves. The Heisler was an oddity because Meadow River had installed a Worthington feedwater heater on it during an overhaul, one of the few geared locomotives so equipped.

Unfortunately, by the time this author first came upon it in 1957, Rainelle was no longer major league. It was more the Toledo Mudhens of logging, to continue the baseball analogy. The only locomotives on the property were Shays Nos. 1, 5, and 7, and Heisler No. 6, and the only engine that ever seemed to operate when we were around was No. 6, which went on to some degree of fame when sold to the state for use on the Cass Scenic Railroad (Shay No. 7 had already gone to Cass two years earlier).

Alas, in those days the nearby Buffalo Creek & Gauley with 50-car steam-powered coal trains held much more fascination for a thirty-ish train watcher than a logging railroad. It is not always easy to get one's priorities straight when thirty-ish.

By 1957 the Raine empire was starting to come unglued. Uncle Tommy had died in 1933 and Uncle Johnny in 1940. At the helm was Howard L. Gray, the Raines' nephew, who had truly come up through the ranks, having started as a saw filer at Meadow River in his youth.

An innoculous-looking pair of GE 70-ton diesel switchers, No. 8 and 9, had appeared in the Rainelle Yard in January 1957. By special design the traction motors in these diesels were elevated above their normal position so they could ford streams like a Shay without stalling. The faithful wondered, with considerable justification in past expereince, if this signified the end of steam operations on one more logging railroad. But Meadow River required three reliable locomotives at all times to cover daily operation and of their five extant steamers, Shay No. 3, was ready for retirement. Additionally, Shay No. 5 was due for retubing in 1957.

The two diesels did not supplant steam however; the Heisler and Shay No. 7 stayed and were used for several more years before being sold for use on the Cass Scenic Railroad in the 1960s.

Meadow River had more serious problems at the time than the arrival of diesels, however. Although it had been a pioneer in many areas of the logging industry, the mill had not been kept abreast of technology, and was a marvel of inefficient and costly operation. The company tried remaining competitive by paying the lowest wages in the West Virginia logging industry. In the mid-1960s, mill hands were getting less than $2 an hour for their labor, which even then was not big bucks.

The inevitable happened in 1968 when the mill workers went out on strike. With a second strike secheduled, Meadow River sold out to giant Georgia-Pacific. The mill operated through the end of 1970, but after closing for Christmas it never reopened. The cut timber in the woods was brought by train to the former Meadow River Mill Yard, but was off-loaded by truck for transport to a new mill being built by Georgia-Pacific near Rainelle. It is said that the final logging train back to Rainelle derailed ingloriously after the dump crew and sawyers had gone off duty for the last time. The forlorn log cars, still loaded, then sat on a siding next to the mill pond for months awaiting completion of the new mill.

Rather than lay out the capital to modernize the old mill, the entire plant was dismantled and by 1975 not a vestige of it remained. During the dismantling process, a third diesel, 75-ton Porter No. 10, operated at Rainelle and steam was finally absent from Meadow River. Thus ended what had become West Virginia's last rail logging operation.

Georgia-Pacific presently operates a single-band mill with a modest capacity of 15.5 million board feet per year, just outside Rainelle, and all logs come via truck. The log cars, diesel loader and rail-mounted skidder No. 1 are presently at Cass. Today almost all traces of the original Sewell Valley line are gone; the former Loop & Lookout and Greenbrier & Eastern tracks are still a part of the NF&G, but the NF&G is primarily a coal-hauling railroad. A shopping center sits on the site of the rambling old mill. It's doubtful that Uncle Tommy and Uncle Jimmy would have approved!

William E. Warden

Meadow River Lumber Co. caboose No. 3 found a new home at the Cass Scenic Railroad and is shown at that location, lettered for its former owner, in 1973. It was originally a C&O car.

Philip Bagdon

Meadow River had a railbus, too, although its purpose in life is not clear—probably transporting wood hicks and supplies to the logging camp back in the woods. The Kalamazoo Railbus M-4 is shown here at Cass on 1970 after it was donated to the scenic railroad by Georgia-Pacific. It was subsequently damaged and scrapped before being put to use.

Locomotives of Meadow River Lumber Company

No.	Type	Date	BP (psi)	Driver size	Cylinder size	C/N	Previous Owners
1	Shay/2-truck - 42 tons	1910	200	29.5	10x12	2317	Purchased new
2	Shay/3-truck - 70 tons	1911	200	36	12x15	2435	Purchased new
3	Shay/3-truck - 70 tons	1913	200	36	12x15	2686	Purchased new
4	Shay/2-truck - 50 tons	1909	200	32	11x12	2184	Sewell Valley No. 1
5	Shay/3-truck - 70 tons	1923	200	36	12x15	3247	Winchester & Western No. 4
6	Heisler/3-truck - 90 tons	1929	200	40	18x16	1591	Bostonia Coal & Clay Products No. 20
7	Shay/3-truck - 70 tons	1920	200	36	12x15	3131	Raine Lbr. Co. No. 3
8	G. E. Diesel/70 tons	1957	NA	--	NA	32815	Purchased New
9	G. E. Diesel/70 tons	1957	NA	--	NA	32816	Purchased new
10	Porter Diesel/80 tons	1947	NA	--	NA	8160	Philip Carey Mfg. Co. No. 11 P. W. Duffy & Son (to Meadow River in 1956)

Dispositions

Number	Subsequent Owners/final disposition
1	To Steamtown in 1959
2	Scrapped
3	Dismantled for parts in 1958
4	to Birmingham Rail & Locomotive Co. (1942); to Georgia Car & Locomotive No. 612; to Trego Stone Corp. No. 4; scrapped in 1952
5	To Twin Seams Mining Co. No. 5; scrapped in 1963
6	To Cass Scenic Railroad No. 6 in 1966
7	To Cass Scenic Railroad No. 7 in 1964
8	To Continental Grain, Norfolk, Va. in 1975
9	To Crucible Steel (for parts) in 1975
10	Transferred to Georgia-Pacific, Plaquemines, Louisana; scrapped 1976

Legend
C/N - Construction serial number assigned by builder.
BP - Boiler pressure is pounds per square inch.
Cylinder size - Diameter of cylinder and length of piston stroke, in inches.

John B. Allen, Thomas Lawson, Jr. Coll.

Roster by Thomas Lawson, Jr.

Meadow River Shay No. 1, its first locomotive, purchased in 1910, was typical of smaller Shays, shown here at Rainelle in September 1955 sporting a huge balloon stack. Note the pipe at the stack's base for emptying cinders trapped by the spark arresting baffles inside.

Meadow River Shay No. 5 poses at the Rainelle Yard in September 1955, with the imposing skyline of the mill plant behind it. Less than two and a half years later No. 5 was sold to Twin Seams Mining Company where it was scrapped in 1963. The locomotive was purchased new from Lima by Winchester & Western in December 1923, as its No. 4. It was the youngest of the Shays on the Meadow River roster.

J. B. Allen, Thomas Lawson, Jr. Coll.

An anachronism in September 1963, Meadow River Shay No. 7 and log loader sit silently in the RainelleYard near the mill's locomotive and machine shop (the white building in the background). They had outlasted the overwhelming majority of their kind and awaited their own fate—No. 7 escaped the scrapper and is now working for the Cass Scenic Railroad.

Philip Bagdon

William E. Warden

The mill at Rainelle is shut down for the last time when this photo was taken in April 1971, as the last of the finished lumber in the huge storage yard is being transferred to waiting flat cars for shipment.

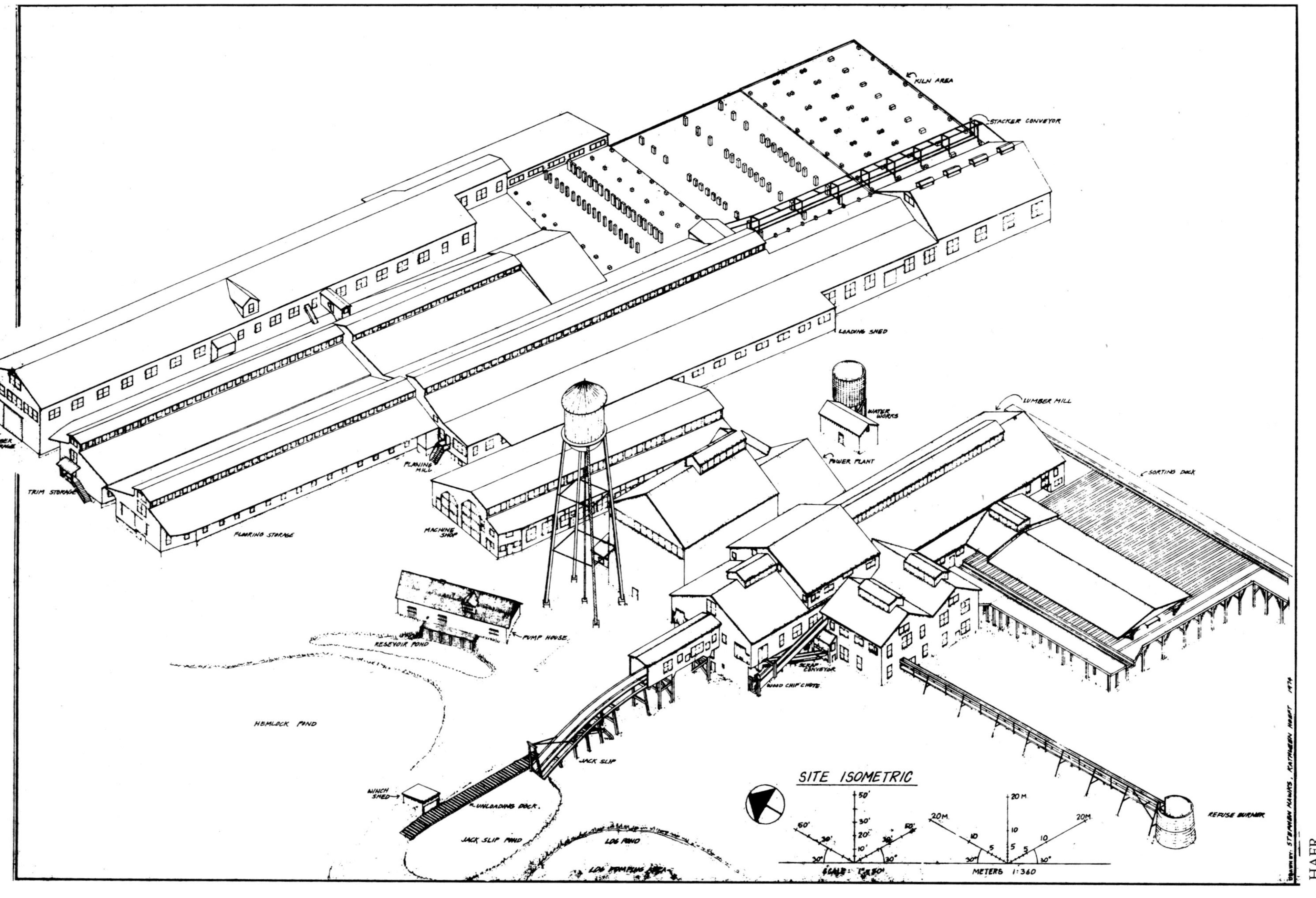

This drawing of the Meadow River Lumber Co.Mill at Rainelle was done as part of a survey of the site by the Historic American Engineering Record just before the mill's demolition. The sawmill itself is the structure at the lower right of the drawing. The machine/locomotive shop and power house are between it and the huge lumber storage sheds and kilns. Unfortunately the railroad tracks were not included in this drawing. That this was one of the largest of sawmills is evident in this drawing and the photo on the facing page.

C&O Historical Society Coll.

Acres and acres of cut and stacked hardwood lumber on the docks (center) waiting to be shipped almost anywhere. This aerial view of the Meadow River complex was taken in 1952. The huge finished lumber sheds and kilns are dominant feature to the right, while the mill is to the left and the log ponds beyond that. Just beyond the ponds, hardly visible, is the NF&G Yard and engine facility, while the town of Rainelle is to the right. Today a large shopping center is situated where the lumber yard was.

Train watchers question the crew about one of Meadow River's most recent acquisitions, diesel switcher No. 9, in March 1960. Internal combustion has not totally supplanted steam by this date, though, as the logger's Heisler and Shay are still on the property.

William E. Warden

(Right) Help is on the way. Meadow River Shay No. 3, near Anjean, is on errand of mercy with mechanics on caboose platform to perform some minor surgery on Shay No. 5 which is ailing at Williamfield, in the summer of 1956.

John Krause

(Below) Shay No. 3 ambles across a creek near logging camp No. 104 in October 1956. The wooden trestle is actually a very substantial structure for a logging road. Elk River Coal & Lumber Company would have forded this stream, but Meadow River seems to be a classier operation in this regard.

August A. Thieme

Like some mammonth brooding spider, a Lidgerwood skidder towers over Meadow River Shay No. 5, some logging flats, and a log loader near Anjean in 1957. This photo allows a rather complete view of a skidder, with its enclosed steam engine. If you look closely you can see that it's mounted on a railroad car for easy movement as well.

John Krause

Bernard J. Kern, Philip Bagdon Coll.

(Left) This formidable-looking log loader was scratch built by Meadow River Lumber, and is in the woods eight miles notheast of Anjean. It's obviously made from a railroad crane built to handle much heavier loads than these logs—compare it with other log loaders in this book. This loader was subsequently donated to the Cass Scenic Railroad.

(Below) Coming home to Rainelle with a full load, Meadow River Shay No. 5 is at Rupert on the mainline of the NF&G. Meadow River's logging lines branches off from the common-carrier NF&G which was not even owned by the Raines after 1930. Log trains had trackage rights granted by NF&G's C&O/NYC owners.

Some of Meadow River Lumber Company's camp cars parked at Rainelle after logging was over, in August 1971. Unlike most logging operations Meadow River had camp cars. Others used portable housing, but it wasn't usually built on railroad frames.

Philip Bagdon

(Left) Shay No. 3 has just transferred a crew of mechanics from Rainelle who rode up in caboose to do some field repairs on No. 5 north of Anjean in the summer of 1956. One of the mechanics is on No. 3's running board, but we can't determine the nature of the repairs that required this special assistance.

(both) John Krause

(Below) Deep in the forest near Anjean in 1956, a borrowed C&O flat car is used as an idler for the tree-length logs. Note the rails laid on the flat car for the log loader to move during loading. Only younger trees are left standing on the logged-out hillside. They will grow and spread out and be ready to harvesting in 30-40 years. Alas the little train won't be there to carry them away.

William E. Warden

Heisler No. 6 steams softly in the afternoon sunlight of a cold November day in 1961 just outside the machine shop at Rainelle. This locomotive has gained a measure of fame since its addition to the Cass Scenic Railroad roster in 1966.

Shay No. 3 and caboose have brought a track gang into the woods near Anjean in March 1956. From the look of things they are removing a line immediately behind the train. There is another track curving to the right to another part of the woods. Here again the land has been worked bare of harvestable trees, with only the younger ones left.

William E. Warden

John Krause

Meadow River Heisler No. 6 was sold to the state of West Virginia for use on the Cass Scenic Railroad, and in an unusual operation made its way under its own power down the the NF&G to the C&O mainline at Meadow Creek, thence to Ronceverte, where it took the C&O's Greenbrier branch up to Cass. Days don't get much colder than this in West Virginia, but at least it had been better weather the day before when No. 6 left Rainelle. Here on December 15, 1968, the Heisler puts on a great winter showing on the Greenbrier branch amid a snowfall of some 15 inches that almost stalled the faithful who were following to photograph the move.

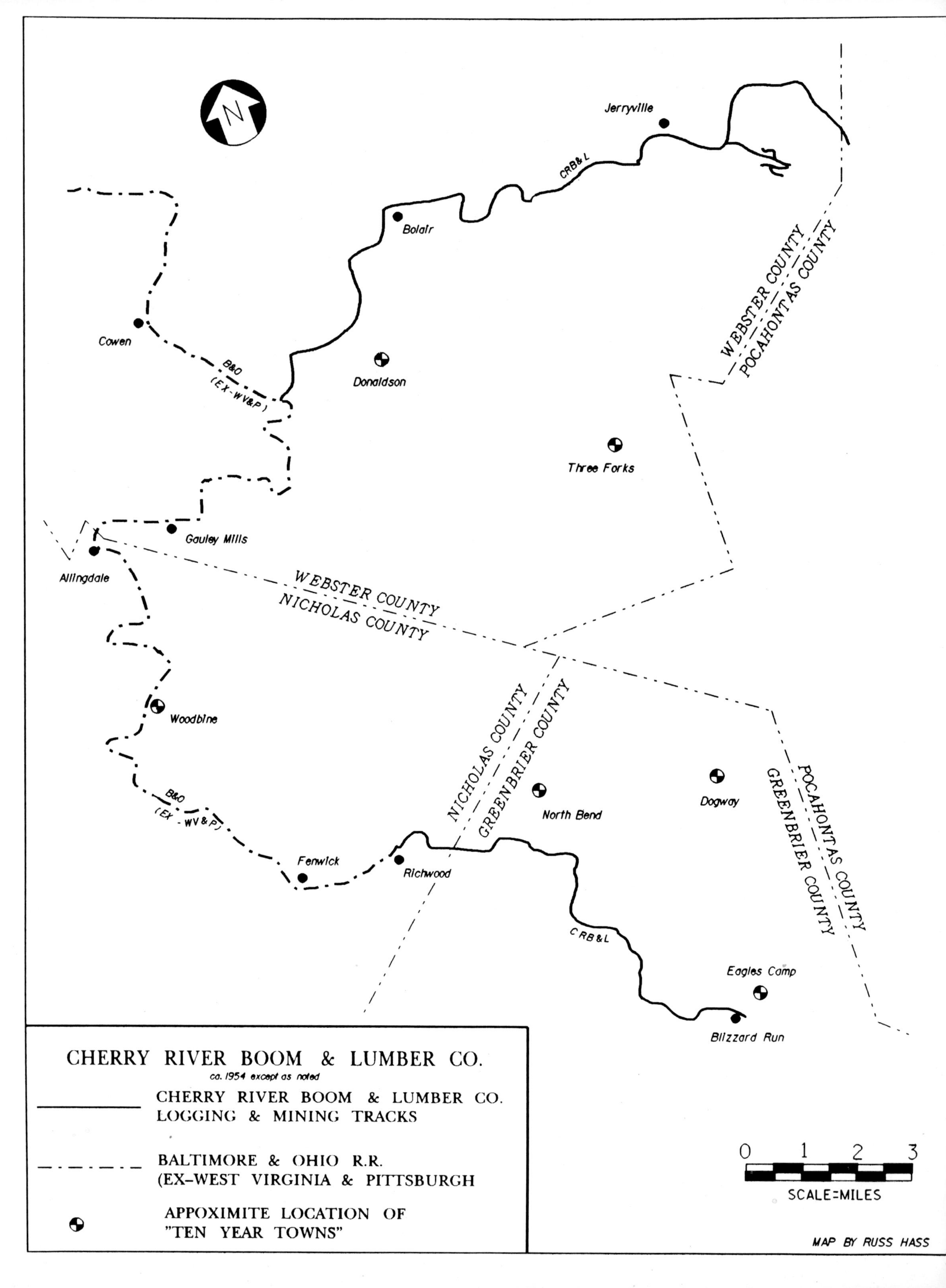

Jerryville
CRB&L
Bolair
Cowen
Donaldson
B&O
(EX-WV&P)
WEBSTER COUNTY
POCAHONTAS COUNTY
Three Forks
Gauley Mills
Allingdale
WEBSTER COUNTY
NICHOLAS COUNTY
Woodbine
NICHOLAS COUNTY
GREENBRIER COUNTY
North Bend
Dogway
POCAHONTAS COUNTY
GREENBRIER COUNTY
B&O
(EX - WV & P)
Fenwick
Richwood
CRB&L
Eagles Camp
Blizzard Run
CHERRY RIVER BOOM & LUMBER CO.
ca. 1954 except as noted
CHERRY RIVER BOOM & LUMBER CO.
LOGGING & MINING TRACKS
BALTIMORE & OHIO R.R.
(EX-WEST VIRGINIA & PITTSBURGH
APPOXIMITE LOCATION OF
"TEN YEAR TOWNS"
0 1 2 3
SCALE=MILES
MAP BY RUSS HASS

Chapter 6 – Cherry River Boom & Lumber Company (Richwood, Nicholas County)

We've already seen how interwoven West Virginia common carrier railroads were with logging operations, so it should come as no surprise to find that one of the state's largest logging operations—and one of its longest-lived--Cherry River Boom & Lumber Company, began life as a common carrier railroad. Sort of.

It started with West Virginia's U. S. Senator Johnson N. Camden, who incorporated the West Virginia & Pittsburgh Railroad (a conglomoration of several narrow-gauge shortlines) in the 1870s. Plans for this grandiosely-named rail line included tracks through the Elk, Greenbrier, and Gauley River Valleys. A connection with the Chesapeake & Ohio main line was to be made via the Cherry or Williams River. Furthermore, it was anticipated that the C&O would extend its Hot Springs, Virginia Branch across the Alleghanies to Marlington where it would connect with the WV&P. Early maps showed Marlinton as the junction of the C&O, WV&P and four other railroads!

Harold K. Vollrath Coll.

Fat-boilered 2-8-2 No. 3 was used to haul Cherry River Boom & Lumber logging trains over B&O rails to Richwood. This was the second CRB&L locomotive numbered 3. It was originally built as Sewell Valley No. 11, and was sold to CRB&L when the C&O took over the NF&G at Rainelle. It was actually a C&O engine for a while under No. 2913.

If this scheme seems a tad far fetched, remember that railroad land promoters at that time were not constrained by laws or good taste from inserting a bit of hyperbole in their advertising. The April 1891 issue of *Railroad Gazette* in fact noted that "C&O...engineers have commenced a survey at the mouth of Cedar Creek...where the Warm Springs Branch leaves the Jackson River, which is to extend to the West Virginia line and which will, when completed, establish a connection with the West Virginia and Pittsburgh."

However, anyone who, in the 1990s, has traversed the hairpin curves and sawtooth profile of Virginia and West Virginia Route 39 from Warm Springs to Marlinton can appreciate that there was little liklihood of the C&O tunneling through Alleghanies between these communities. The wonder is that the WV&P actually did lay track (177 miles by 1879) and run trains. It was leased by the Baltimore & Ohio in 1890 and finally absorbed by the larger road in 1899. That same year the West Virgina & Pittsburgh reached Richwood.

Camden may not have sold many people on his scheme but he did impress John T. McGraw, who had been acquiring timber and mineral rights in Nicholas and Greenbrier counties since 1883. If the chronicles are to be believed, McGraw was a 19th Century T. Boone Pickens and while leveraged buyouts were not popular in the 1890s, McGraw quickly bought up large tracts of land west of Marlinton in Pocahontas County, when he learned of Camden's scheme.

What sort of deal Camden and McGraw worked out is not clear. We do know, however, that this shortline railroad, the West Virginia & Pittsburgh, came to own 135,000 acres in Nicholas, Webster, and Greenbrier Counties, much of it originally McGraw's property. And we further know that in 1907 this vast holding was deeded to Scranton, Pennsylvania-based Cherry River Boom & Lumber Company, which already owned some 40,000 acres along Little Laurel Creek and the North and South Forks of the Cherry River.

While the C&O couldn't provide an outlet for Cherry River's production, the B&O could. In August 1900, the B&O and Cherry River Boom and Lumber Company entered into an agreement whereby logging trains would be allowed to ride on B&O rails and the railroad would charge no more than a maximum fixed rate for hauling Cherry River's output to Philadelphia. Additionally, the B&O agreed to supply at no charge rails for constructing logging lines. In return CRB&L agreed to erect a mill at the forks of the Cherry River (present-day Richwood) that would guarantee 50 million board feet of business to the B&O per year.

Cherry River Boom & Lumber, as we have said before, was one of the biggest logging operations in the state–maybe even the biggest east of the Mississippi, if you accept some reports–with a mill capacity of 175,000 feet per day in 1917, and cut timber along both forks of the Cherry River, plus the Gauley, Cranberry and Williams Rivers. At one time ten Shays and nine rod locomotives plus four log loaders and a host of flat cars, hoppers (CRB&L had its own coal mining operation), railbuses to transport wood hicks, and tank cars of water to take care of trackside fires, plied a spiderweb of 142 miles of track, much of it connected to Richwood by the B&O. Beginning with the earliest days of operation, some important threads in this web included:

Railroad Museum of Pennsylvania

One of Cherry River Boom & Lumber railbuses, No. D-4, used to transport wood hicks and miners from Richwood to their jobs, parked amid the industrial clutter characteristic of the era.

Richwood to Elk Lick
Richwood to North Bend and Dogway
Allingdale to Donaldson
Donaldson to Three Forks
Donaldson to Jerryville
Woodbine to Dogway
Richwood to Eagles Cup
Richwood to Blizzard Run

The last-named branch, on the South Fork of the Cherry River, was only opened in 1952 and logging continued on it until the end of rail operations.

The company ultimately owned over 200,000 acres (some reports say almost 300,000)–313 square miles, more that the combined area of several West Virginia counties––of virgin timber in the above mentioned counties.

Some time before 1900, the CRB&L erected a small circular sawmill for purpose of building an immense bandsaw and planning mill complex at the junction of the North and South Forks of Cherry River. B&O's branch line, incorporating portions of the West Virginia & Pittsburgh, reached the point where the two forks came together by the spring of 1901. Ready for the railroad, in accordance with the 1900 agreement, was the "Big Mill" which supplanted the smaller circular sawmill. At its top production in 1929, this mill's output was 250,000 board feet daily, considerably more feet per year.

The first Cherry River board was sawed on July 25, 1901. Then almost as an afterthought, the community springing up around the mill was incorporated on November 3 of that year and aptly named Richwood. Unlike most West Virginia mill towns, Richwood, as well as housing the sawmill and car shops (which could almost build a locomotive from scratch and did perform light engine repairs for B&O until it built a shop of its own at Cowen), attracted a number of small industries related to lumbering. By 1914 products as diverse as broom handles (there is still a piece of land at Richwood named Handle Factory Hollow), leather soles (at one time the Richwood tannery was reputedly the largest sole leather tannery in the world), clothespins, and wooden dishes were shipped out of Richwood on the B&O.

Lumber provided the bulk of the carloadings with CRB&L shipping as many as 4,000 carloads per year of spruce and hemlock lumber. But at the same time, the B&O was taking delivery of 330 cars of clothespins and 240 cars of wooden dishes per year. Population grew to 7,000 people at Richwood's peak—down to just 4,100 in 1960––and it became a raucous town like many another in the state.

Lumbering was Cherry River's big business and the coal mines sort of mooched along minding their own business (the opposite of the Elk River Coal and Lumber's philosophy) while supplying coal to the B&O for its locomotives, plus CRB&L mills and locomotives, until the Depression. Not much building was going on in the 1930s and of course those small industries at Richwood were devastated too. Mill production was down to 40 million board feet per year by the mid-1930s and trackage had shrunk to 75 miles. But coal was still the heating fuel of choice in most cities and towns and it still fired most of the country's electric power plants. Hence, mine production kept the company solvent in those lean years.

Nothing particularly noteworth here, and Cherry River's coal transportation operation might have faded unremarked into oblivion if it hadn't been for a coal mine strike at Jerryville in 1954. Ostensibly, the strike was called in an attempt to unionize a J. R. Maust Coal & Coke strip mining operation. Striking miners did not necessarily play by Marquis of Queensbury rules and, to get Maust's attention, bombed one of CBR&L's bridges in September 1954, possibly in imitation of the recent strike against Elk River Coal & Lumber. The bridge was repaired and reopened on October 19, 1954. The first coal train was scheduled for the following day.

Rumors of further trouble were plentiful around Richwood and Jerryville on October 20th. State police were patroling a nearby highway and a Jeep "hi-railer" with two armed guards aboard had been sent on ahead of the coal train to scout the track. The guards reported nothing suspicious, but a crude booby trap had been placed on the track at Millers Mill Run between Jerryville and Bolair. The trap was to be triggered by a fishing line strung between two trees. The line was high enough up so it would be above the roof of the Jeep but low enough to snag the steam engine's stack. The wire in turn was connected to a mouse trap and the trap, when closed would complete an electrical circuit between a battery and a considerable quantity of dynamite buried beneath the track.

When the 39-car train's locomotive reached the run, the booby trap exploded, overturning the locomotive, tender, and one hopper car. Two other hoppers were derailed. Fireman Robert Nichols, seeing his engine turning over, tried to jump clear of it but was caught by one of the derailed hoppers and crushed to death. He was the only fatality.

Unlike in the case of the Elk River strike, state police reacted almost immediately. Four suspects were rounded up and given lie detector tests. However they were inconclusive and, lacking any other evidence, the police were forced to free the men. Ultimately three miners were tried in federal district court for the bombing, convicted and each given a 20-year prison sentence.

It's unclear as to which locomotive was bombed. One school of thought is that it was No. 482, Cherry River's heaviest 2-8-2. Another claims that it was the lightweight No. 15, but trainwatcher John Allen photographed this locomotive in service some two years after the bombing incident; besides, it would have been rather light for hauling coal drags. A third theory is that it was No. 3, but this locomotive was shipped to Glassport, Pennsylvania, for scrapping in 1957, so it was at least road worthy three years after the bombing. (If it was the bombed locomotive, No. 3 may have suffered only minimal damage of course.) Finally, a fourth school postulates that it had to be No. 26. All four versions have vociferous partisans. Contemporary newspaper accounts refer to it only as a "96-ton locomotive." Readers may feel free to take sides, although this writer is inclined to think No. 3 was the most likely victim.

By the 1950s, when train watchers began paying attention to logging roads, Cherry River's empire had shrunk considerably with production running in the neighborhood of 15 million board feet per year. Back in 1933 the company had sold 153,000 acres of cutover land to the U. S. Forest Service, which proceeded to create from it much of the present-day Monongahela National Forest. Logging was centered around Jerryville–named in typical West Virginia fashion for woods boss Jerry Webb Hollifield–Bolair, and Three Forks.

When Cherry River acquired the Camden properties, the company also took possession of two other band mills, one at Gauley Mills and the other at Holcomb. The fact that only connection between Richwood and logging territory, as well as the band mill at Gauley Mills, was over 19 miles of B&O branch line may account for why Cherry River, unlike other West Virginia loggers, relied heavily on rod locomotives to power its logging trains. And what logging trains they were!

Typically in the 1950s an elderly 2-8-2, riding on 90-pound rail, and under the command of engineer Criss Thompson or Manse Williams and conductor Jimmy Shuttlesworth or Bill Jones might come chuffing into Richwood around 4:00 p.m. with 30-40 logging flats in tow. (A 67-car logging train on the CRB&L has been reported.) A second train of similar consist would arrive in Richwood two hours later. As you probably suspect, this was not just a day's cut at one location but rather what was picked up at four or five different locations where Shays and log loaders had been busy all day–in some cases for several days. Like Meadow River, Cherry River Boom & Lumber believed in leaving its logging equipment out in the woods overnight. Unlike Meadow River, however, it did not have portable logging camps and thus the railbuses provided the necessary commuter service for the loggers after logging camps became passe.

Somewhat incongruously, Cherry River in the mid-1950s still used an occasional team of horses to skid logs!

This happy state of affairs, with 70-ton General Electric diesels retiring the last of the steamers in 1955,* continued until 1959, at which time the entire logging operation (much reduced in size as land was logged out) was sold to W. M. Ritter. Ritter in turn, as we have seen elsewhere in this book, was merged into giant Georgia-Pacific in 1960.

Today Georgia-Pacific operates a modern electric band mill, producing 65,000 board feet of lumber per day at Richwood, all logs brought in by trucks. The diesels were retired in 1968 and sold and few people remember the logging trains.

---

*Two of the Shays, Nos. 2 and 7, were sold to the Elk River Coal & Lumber Co. It is said that when the locomotives left Richwood, people from every house along the track came out to wave farewell to them!

If No. 482 looks out of place on a logging railroad, well it should. It was built for mainline service on the Mobile & Ohio in 1928, and came to CRB&L in 1950. It was used primarily to haul the company's heavy coal trains. Seen here at Jerryville in 1950, five years before it was scrapped.

Charles E. Winters

Locomotives of Cherry River Boom & Lumber Company

No.	Type	Date	BP (psi)	Driver size	Cylinder size/stroke	C/N	Previous Owners
1(1st)	Shay/3-truck-50-ton	1901	180	32	12.5x12	635	Purchased new
1(2nd)	Shay/3-truck-70-ton	1913	200	36	12x15	2695	Andrews Lbr. Co. (No. 2)
1(3rd)	G. E. Diesel/70-ton	1954	NA	—	NA	32278	Purchased new
2(1st)	Shay/2-truck-50-ton	1901	180	32	12.5x12	661	Purchased new
2(2nd)	Shay3-truck-65-ton	1905	?	36	12x15	1568	Tioga Lbr. Co. (No. 2) Birch Valley Lbr. Co. (No. 2)
2(3rd)	G. E. Diesel/70-ton	1955	NA	—	NA	32279	Purchased new
3(1st)	0-4-4 Forney	1878	?	38	10x14	4484	Manhattan Railway (No. 76) Cherry River Tanning Co.
3(2nd)	2-8-2 (Baldwin)	1922	?	?	20x28	55622	Sewell Valley (No. 11) Chesapeake & Ohio (No. 2913) Birmingham Rail & Loco (No. 659)
3(3rd)	G. E. Diesel/70-ton	1956	NA	—	NA	32682	Purchased new
4	Shay/3-truck-50-ton	1902	?	32	12x12	746	Purchased new
5	2-8-0 (Cooke)	1885	?	?	20x24	1638	Detroit Southern (No. 25) Detroit, Toledo & Ironton (No.25) Cherry River Paper Co.
6	Shay/3-truck-85-ton	1904	?	40	14.5x15	742	Purchased new
7	Shay/3-truck-65-ton	1904	?	36	12x15	916	Clover Run Lbr. Co. (No. 7)
8	Shay/3-truck-50-ton	1902	?	33	12x12	735	James Strong Lbr. Co. (No. 3)
9(1st)	2-6-0 (Baldwin)	1913	?	?	?	40949	Purchased new (originally an 0-6-0)
9(2nd)	2-6-0 (Baldwin)	1916	?	?	16x24	44502	Purchased new
9(3rd)	2-6-0 (Note 1)	?	?	?	?	—	Built by CRB&L (see Note 1)
10	Shay/3-truck-65-tons	1905	?	36	12x15	971	Baltimore & Ohio (No.1)
11	Shay/3-truck-70-tons	1906	?	36	12x15	1648	Purchased new
12	Shay/3-truck-65-tons	1906	?	36	12x15	1649	Purchased new
14	Shay/3-truck-80-tons	1911	200	36	13.5x15	2440	Purchased new
15	2-8-2 (Baldwin/Note 2)	1912	?	?	?	37809	Purchased new
16	Shay/3-truck-68-ton	1906	?	32	12x15	1799	Enterprise Lbr. Co. (No. 4)
17	Shay/3-truck-90-ton	1916	200	40	14.5x15	2863	Purchased new
18	2-8-0 (Baldwin)	1915	?	?	?	42076	Mt. Hope Mineral (No. 3) E. H. Wilson Co. (dealer) Birmingham Rail & Loco Co. in 1929
26	2-8-2 (Baldwin)	1910	?	51	22x28	35263	Woodward Iron Co. (No. 26) Birmingham Rail & Loco. Co. (No. 1771)
482	2-8-2 (Alco) (Schenectady)	1928	200	63	26x30	67568	Mobile & Ohio No. 482 Gulf, Mobile & Ohio (No. 482) GC&L Co. in 1950
—	G. E. Diesel/20-ton	1947	NA	—	NA	?	(Note 3)

Note 1 - Assembled at Richwood shops from parts of other locomotives including tender from first No. 9; identify of other two clouded.
Note 2 - Was built as a 2-8-0; trailing truck probably added by Richwood shops.
Note 3 - May have been converted from narrow gauge to standard for use on CRB&L.

Dispositions

Number	Subsequent owner/disposition
1(1st)	W. Va. Coal & Coke Co.; scrapped at Omar, W. Va. in 1947
1(2nd)	Scrapped about 1947
1(3rd)	Central La Romana, Dominican Republic (No. 25)
2(1st)	W. Va. Coal & Coke Co.; scrapped at Omar, W. Va. in 1947
2(2nd)	Elk River Coal & Lbr. Co. in 1956 (see ERC&L roster on page 50)
2(3rd)	Modesto & Empire Traction Co. (No. 603) in 1968
3(1st)	Off roster by 1929; disposition unknown
3(2nd)	Scrapped at Richwood in 1957
3(3rd)	Central La Romana, Dominican Republic (No. 24)
4	Rowlesburg & Southern RR (No. 4); scrapped at Rowlesburg, W. Va. about 1940
5	Derelect in 1939; disposition unknown
6	Cheat River RR (No. 6); Rowlesburg & Southern (No. 3); scrapped at Rowlesburg about 1940
7	Elk River Coal & Lbr. in 1956 (see ERC&L roster on page 50)
8	Off roster by 1939, disposition unknown
9(1st)	Sold to Birmingham Rail & Loco Co.; scrapped without leaving Richwood
9(2nd)	Georgia Car & Loco. No. 647 in 1929; later Pine Mountain Granite No. 6; disposition unknown
9(3rd)	Georgia Car & Loco. No.671; sold back to CRB&L in 1930 without moving; in service at Richwood in 1939; disposition unknown
10,11,12,14	All off roster by 1939; disposition unknown
15	Scrapped at Richwood in 1959™
16	F. C. Cook & Co. No. 16; Ely-Thomas Lbr. Co. No. 2; now on display ay Pennsylvania State Railroad Museum
17	Twin Seams Mining Co. No. 17 in 1947; scrapped at Kellerman, Alabama in 1963
18	Wrecked on Straight Creek; off roster by 1960
26	Scrapped at Jerryville in 1955
482	Scrapped at Jerryville in 1955
Diesel	To Birmingham Rail & Loco; to Tenneco, Telogia, Florida; scrapped

Legend

C/N - Construction serial number assigned by the builder.
BP - Boiler pressure expressed in pounds per square inch.
Cylinder size/stroke - Diameter of cylinders and length of piston stroke in inches.

Roster by Philip Bagdon

CRB&L Shay No. 4, pictured here after being sold to the Rowlesburg & Southern Railray but still wearing its former owner's huge number on its tank, is very near the end of its life when photographed July 2, 1949, in Erwin, W. Va. The R&S was abandoned the following year and the locomotive scrapped.

F. W. Trittenbach, Thomas Lawson, Jr. Coll.

Former CRB&L Shay No. 17 is shown here decaying on an isolated stretch of track in Kellerman, Alabama, in September 1959. According to the photographer, the lettering for the "Twin Seams Mining Co." was done as a courtesy by the Richwood shops at the time of the locomotive's sale.

(both) Thomas Lawson, Jr.

Three-truck Shay No. 7, at Richwood in August 1956, was typical of older C-Class locomotives. It was later sold to Elk River Coal & Lumber, and scrapped for parts in 1959. It was originally built in 1904 for Clover Run Lumber Company, another West Virginia concern.

The sloped-back tender is a dead giveaway that this stubby 2-6-0 started life as an 0-6-0 switcher. It was Cherry River Boom & Lumber's second No. 9, but was Pine Mountain No. 6 when this 1936 photograph was taken in Lithonia, Georgia.

William Monypeny, Thomas Lawson, Jr. Coll.

CRB&L Mikado (2-8-2) No. 26 sits at Jerryville while awaiting its next assignment in September 1951. It was originally built by Baldwin Locomotive Works for Woodward Iron Co. in Birmingham, Alabama in 1910, and came to CRB&L in 1935.

Charles J. Dengler, William E. Warden Coll.

Sitting quietly outside the CRB&L engine house at Jerryville during Labor Day weekend of 1949 is 2-8-2 No. 3. Is this the Mikado that was bombed in the mineworker's strike? Many people think so. It was originally Sewell Valley Railway No. 11

Charles J. Dengler, Thomas Lawson, Jr. Coll.

This imaginatively remodeled CRB&L box car-cum-caboose still retained its logging railroad arch bar trucks, but had outlived its usefulness in this July 1959 photo. Two log loaders hover protectively over this idiosyncratic crummy in the Richwood Yard. Logging truck in the background between the caboose and the loaders is an omen.

William E. Warden

Slide-valved No. 3 poses at Jerryville in August 1952. Whether No. 3 is ready to take the log loader at right into the woods or haul one of Cherry River's coal trains we don't know. The engine house in the background has an oddly shaped door, probably a necessity when taller spark arresters were in position atop locomotive stacks.

William E. Warden

Richard J. Cook, Sr.

Shay No. 2, lately from the Cherry River Boom & Lumber Company, is about to be reborn as No. 19 of the Elk River Coal and Lumber Co. The Shay had just recently arrived at Dundon when this photo was taken in July 1957, and had not yet been renumbered and put into service.

CRB&L Shay No. 7 and crew seem to be posing for a family portrait. More likely however, men and machine are waiting for another train to clear the siding at the left in this July 1956 photo. Three other men are moving some boards around on the flatcars behind.

(both William E. Warden

(Below) These snub-nosed railbuses, property of CRB&L, wait stoically in the Richwood Yard, a reminder of an age when wood hicks were transported to the logging sites and coal miners to the mine in these conveyances.

(three photos) John Krause

(Above, left) CRB&L Shay No. 7 has just picked up some empty flat cars and is somewhere near the South Fork of the Cherry River in search of logs to fill them. Of interest is that the fact that the track here has tie plates under its rails, contrary to usual logging railroad practice. ***(Above, right)*** No. 7 is again looking for logs, this time near Blizzard Run in the mid-1950s. ***(Left)*** CRB&L 2-8-2 No. 15 powers a log train in the mid-1950s. The log loader sits atop rickety flat cars fitted out with track for the loader to move along as it picks up logs and deposits them in the car ahead.

Richard J. Cook, Sr.

Mikado No. 3 here is chuffing through Cowen on the Baltimore & Ohio's tracks with some logging cars in June of 1947.

Cherry River Shay No. 7 is tiptoeing through the woods near Jerryville in the summer of 1956. Note the pile of logs just to the right of the pilot, probably to be picked up by this train.

(both) John Krause

Baldfaced 2-8-2 No. 15 is working a log train, the loader picking up logs that have been skidded to trackside. CRB&L's rod locomotive usually just hauled already loaded flats back to the Richwood mill so this operation with one on a logging train is unusual. Note the spark arrester atop No. 15's stack.

It seems unlikely that even a Shay could navigate the track we see here, but it is crudely laid light rail on top of flat cars to be used by the log loader as it moves along the train loading logs. Stakes for the pole pockets on the sides of the cars are laid across the cars making their appearance even less inviting. No. 15, at right, has flats on both ends, a loader in process of hoisting logs on those to the rear.

(both) John Krause

Here No. 15 is in the middle of its train, having apparently picked up the cars on the siding in the photo above and put them on its rear. Just where the two cars being loaded in the other photo have gone is guess-work, but they may now be behind the box car, out of the photo.

William E. Warden

In 1951, No. 15 is off to work on the CRB&L's Richwood Yard, as it assembles a cut of empty logging flats. The 15 will deliver them to one of the logging sites. A log loader is partially visible just to the left of the boiler and stack.

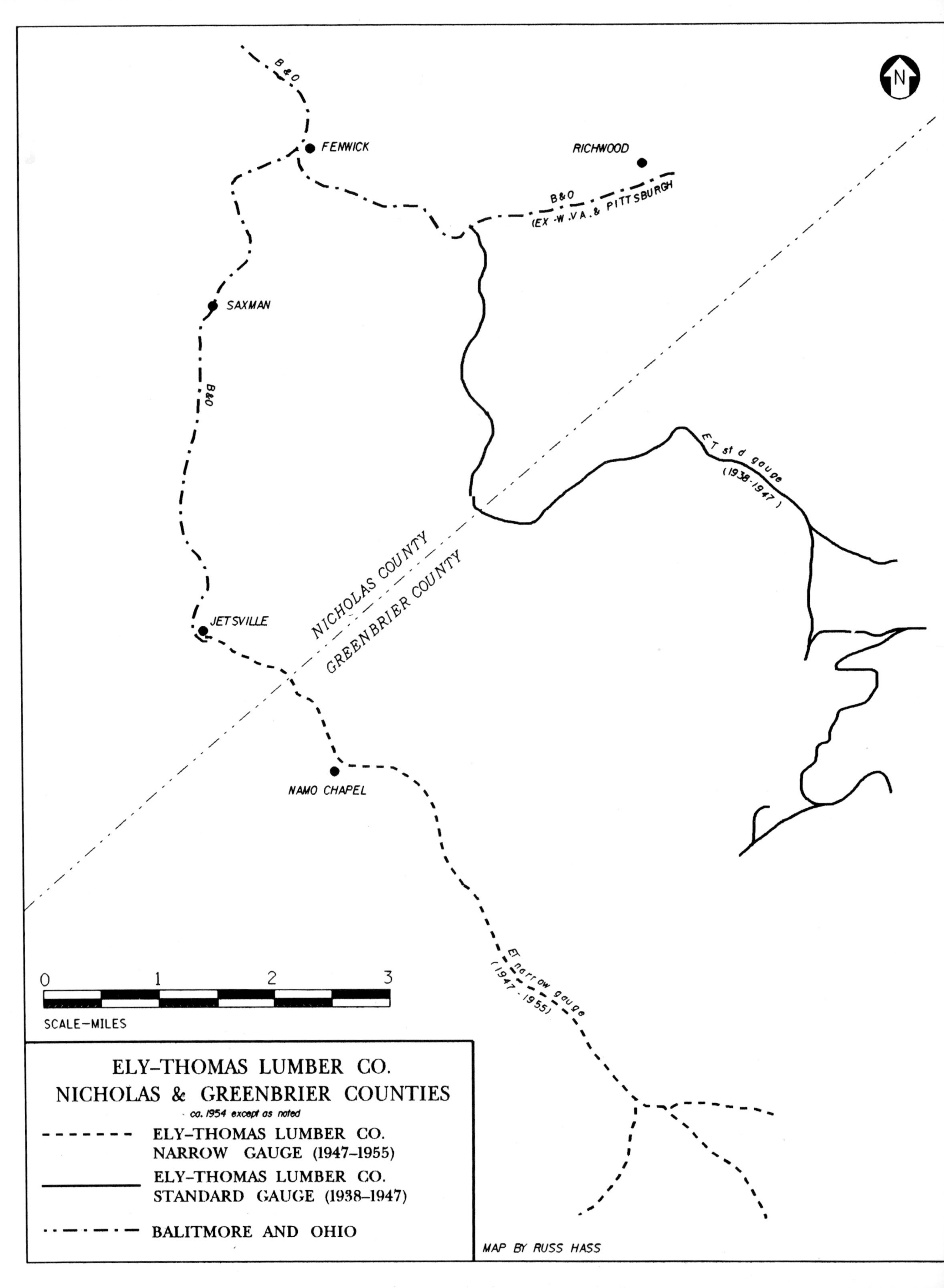

B&O
FENWICK
RICHWOOD
B&O
(EX-W.VA.& PITTSBURGH
SAXMAN
B&O
ET std gauge
(1938-1947)
NICHOLAS COUNTY
GREENBRIER COUNTY
JETSVILLE
NAMO CHAPEL
ET narrow gauge
(1947-1955)
0
1
2
3
SCALE-MILES
ELY-THOMAS LUMBER CO.
NICHOLAS & GREENBRIER COUNTIES
ca. 1954 except as noted
ELY-THOMAS LUMBER CO.
NARROW GAUGE (1947–1955)
ELY-THOMAS LUMBER CO.
STANDARD GAUGE (1938–1947)
BALITMORE AND OHIO
MAP BY RUSS HASS

Chapter 7 – Ely-Thomas Lumber Company (Fenwick, Nicholas County)

Wander along West Virginia Route 39 about three miles west of Richwood and you come to Fenwick, home of the new kid on the block in West Virginia logging, Ely-Thomas Lumber Company, whose corporate history dates back only to 1938. But if Ely-Thomas was a logging upstart, it was a colorful one and in its halcyon days could boast of a schizophrenic Shay, both narrow and standard gauge tracks, and a locomotive fireman and general jack-of-all-trades nicknamed "Poop." More on Poop, the schizoid locomotive, and the two gauges in a moment. But first some history.

Around the turn of the century, the Fenwick Lumber Company built a band mill at the confluence of the Cherry River, Cedar Creek (Big Cedar Creek on some maps), and the B&O's Richwood Subdivision from Cowen, the same branch that served the Cherry River Boom & Lumber Company, and which had originally been built by the West Virginia & Pittsburgh. The town of Fenwick sprang up around the mill.

As a corporate entity Fenwick Lumber seems to have vanished from Nicholas County in the late 1920s. Pete Eakin's Eakin Lumber Company, which already had cut timber in other parts of the state, built a new steam-powered single-band mill at Fenwick in 1927 or 1928. Eakin began logging hardwood along Little Laurel Creek, which flows into the Cherry River between Fenwick and Richwood. Logs came out of the woods on a standard-gauge log train powered by a three-truck Shay that ultimately became Ely-Thomas No. 3. Eakin's rail operation is said to have peaked at around 40 miles of track.

The Great Depression finally doomed Eakin Lumber. In 1938 the Fenwick mill and Eakin's railroad equipment were purchased by lumber barons Ralph Ely and Wellington "Bull" Thomas and thus was born Ely-Thomas Lumber Comapny. It is said that the value of the six or seven million board feet of hardwood lumber in the mill yard was sufficient to recoup the price Ely and Thomas paid for Eakin's entire Fenwick operations.

Initially, it appears that E-T continued logging along Little Laurel. But in 1947 Ely-Thomas built an18-mile, 3-foot gauge logging spur from Jetsville into dense forests and high mountains to the south and southeast. B&O already had a spur from Fenwick through the flyspeck of Saxman to Jetsville to serve one or more coal mines along Laurel Creek south of Fenwick. According to one story, either Eakin or Fenwick Lumber had originally built this line and later sold it to the B&O but this author tends to doubt that, since there is no evidence that either company was engaged in coal mining. There is some evidence, however, that Cherry River Boom & Lumber may have built the line originally and sold it to the B&O.

Just where the slim-gauge track went is not clear but it seems likely that it continued to follow Laurel Creek from Jetsville southeasterly into Greenbrier County at least as far as the creek's headwaters about four miles east-southeast of Clearco, and finally ended up in the vicinity of Manns Run. In addition, a short branch line followed Cold Spring Branch. Current topographical maps show a Jeep trail originating near Jetsville and closely paralleling the creek bed. It is likely that the trail was formed from the logging road's right-of-way. Since Meadow River Lumber was logging around Clearco in the 1950s, tracks of the two logging roads must have been within whistle sound of each other.

William E. Warden

Ely-Thomas Shays No. 2 and 3 sit stoically at the Fenwick Yard awaiting an assignment. Slots in the coupler pockets allow the coupler height to be adjusted to whatever is being pulled or pushed.

Veteran train watcher August Thieme of Richmond, Virginia, reports one incident he witnessed that illustrates the informality of the narrow gauge logging operation. It seems that the track crossed a fenced field a mile or so south of Jetsville, and gates had to be opened to permit passage of the train. The field was the site of Namo Chapel, a small country church. One Sunday, while Thieme was aboard the train, there was a church picnic in progress in the field when the train stopped to allow opening the gate. Some of the church members thereupon invited the train crew and their passenger to stay a spell and join the picnic, which the crew and their passenger did--probably one of the few instances of a logging train going to church.

Motive power for the narrow gauge road included a Climax (reputedly the last such narrow-gauge engine in logging service in the United States) and two 2-truck Shays, all equiped with the primitive link-and-pin couplers favored by owners of narrow gauge logging roads. Tracks around the Fenwick mill itself were a standard 4-feet 8-1/2 inches between the railheads. Standard gauge Shays equipped with standard knuckle couplers worked the yard and, on rare occasions, ran on B&O tracks nine miles to pick up logs a Jetsville.

When a narrow gauge locomotive at Jetsville needed repairs and work couldn't be done at the small shop there, the steamer rode aboard the logging company's standard-gauge flat cars in B&O freights back to the Fenwick shops. It is reported that the narrow gauge engines sometimes rode flatbed trucks over the road from Jetsville to Fenwick. Considering the state of this dirt and gravel road it seems unlikely that anything as heavy as a locomotive (even a slim gauge one) would normally have been transported by motor truck. Incidentally, the standard gauge track was considered an "industrial spur" of the B&O and hence it does not show up in any contemporary *Official Guides*, although the latest topographical and county road maps do label it as "Baltimore & Ohio."

Why two gauges? The exact reasons for the narrow gauge are not clear. The need to navigate sharp curves and steep grades on Saxman Hill may have been a factor. Years earlier Ralph Ely operated a narrow gauge Climax near Camden-on-Gauley and his previous experience may have made him partial to slim-gauge tracks. Then too, second-hand narrow gauge locomotives might have been considerably cheaper than standard gauge ones. The fact that narrow gauge road was only put into operation in the 1940s—making it probably the last built-from-scratch narrow gauge road constructed east of the Rocky Mountains—makes a logical explanation even more difficult.

The other question is why use standard gauge tracks and locomotives around the mill itself? The reason was simply that E-T needy to be able to load boxcars and flats of finished lumber at the mill and interchange them with the B&O. Of course the equipment was already there, thanks to Eakin Lumber, and that was no small consideration. Having tracks with two different gauges that were separated by nine miles of common-carrier railroad made logging a time-consuming operation, made even more difficult by the fact that the American model "D" narrow-gauge log loader used was permanently mounted to its own trucks and could not travel along the tops of cars. The narrow-gauge flats themselves were primitive skeleton cars, less than half the length of a standard car.

Standard operating procedure included leaving the log loader on a siding near the logging site until it needed to be returned to Fenwick for repairs. Logging crews were bunked in portable camps out in the woods from Sunday afternoon until Friday. A train consisting of the narrow gauge locomotives running backward and pushing several flat cars left Jetsville around noon each day. When the train reached the aforementioned siding, the loader was cut in behind the locomotive or the first skeleton flat and the assemblage went clanking off to the actual logging site.

Once the site was reached the loader was chocked and chained to the tracks and the locomotive uncoupled. The loader would then pick up the closest empty, swing it around between itself and the locomotive, and proceed to load it. When the car was loaded, the locomotive pulled it forward a car length and the whole process repeated until the entire train was piled with logs.

When the train got back to Jetsville, the cars were unloaded by removing the stakes from pockets in the car sides and the logs rolled onto the ground between the narrow gauge and B&O tracks. A Barnhart loader riding atop standard gauge flat cars was cut into the B&O local and the train, powered by a regular B&O locomotive, chugged back to Fenwick where the log cars were set out. They were then taken by an Ely-Thomas standard gauge Shay to the mill pond for dumping.

William E. Warden

Piles of finished lumber almost dwarf Ely-Thomas Shay No. 2, here puttering around the Fenwick Yard. For once the West Virginia weather is neither cold, nor wet, nor rainy, nor snowy, but what you'd have a right to expect of a fine September day in 1962.

Although the standard gauge Shays continued to putter around the Fenwick mill until the mid-1960s, the narrow gauge operation was discontinued in 1955, a victim of floods that wiped out bridges crossing Laurel Creek plus, at least in part, its own inefficiency. Thereafter trucks brought the cut logs to Fenwick, dumping them on top of a convenient hillside, the mill pond not being accessible by road. The Barnhart loader then picked up the logs from the bottom of the hill and loaded them on standard gauge flat cars. A Shay then trundled this new logging "train" over to the mill pond, just a short distance away.

If all this loading and unloading sounds complicated and time-consuming, that is only because it was.

While Ely-Thomas's logging locations are shrouded in mystery (sort of a woodsy CIA operation that novelist Tom Clancy would have loved), the history of some of its eccentric employees is not.

Henry Hudson "Poop" Dooley (the nickname refers to a certain problem with which Dooley was afflicted) was one of the most colorful logging locomotive firemen in West Virginia history. Rod Neal, who grew up in Fenwick, recalls him thus: "'he was a small wiry man, maybe 150 pounds. [He] seldom bathed or shaved, always had a plug of Mule in his mouth and running down both sides that dried in his beard. He would come to McCoy's Restaurant for a beer after work. He never took the tobacco out of his mouth; drank beer for hours, and never spit–just kept adding little bits of the plug of Mule." "Old Doc" Frame was the company doctor and another colorful character. His standard response to all reported ailments was "Deng dang to hades. I know just how you feel." Old Doc's trademark was a long overcoat that he wore summer and winter and whose pockets were normally loaded with beer bottles.

The schizoid Shay? Well, as West Virginia train watchers in the early 1960s were aware, there were two yard Shays of similar appearance numbered 2 and 3. Sometime in the decade one of the Shays was retired, leaving what appeared to be No. 2 as the survivor. But the survivor was partially No. 3. After retirement, No. 3's tender had been removed and used to replace No. 2's leaky tank. Several train watchers have suggested that the side of No. 2's cab was restencilled with a "3" (improbable) or else that No. 3's tender was restencilled with a "2" (possible) so that the cab number agreed with the tender number. Hence No. 2 was no. 3, or No. 3 was No. 2, or...Well, you get the point.

Whether this swapping of tanks was permanent, or whether it was just a temporary measure until No. 2's tank could be repaired, seems to be a matter of considerable controversy in the West Virginia train watching community. The author would prefer not to take sides here. However, photographs he took of No. 2 in September 1962 and again in September and December 1963, do show it toting No. 3's tender. (No. 3's tender was smooth-sided whereas No. 2's original tender had two rows of rivets on the sides, according to photographs taken in 1958.) What number was on the tender's end at the time and when the swap took place is not known.

Shay No. 3 (the original one) departed for a Pennsylvania logging rail museum in 1964. But Fenwick Yard remained the smoky preserve of No. 2 until the end of 1965, making it the last regularly-operated geared steam locomotive in West Virginia. In the last days of 1965, No. 2 was retired and its duties taken over by a small diesel locomotive.

Several attempts were made by local train watchers and Ely-Thomas management to sell the old stemwinder to the state of West Virginia for the Cass Scenic Railroad. But Cass already had purchased the ex-Meadow River Lumber Shay No. 7 only the previous year and Cass management was not inclined to acquire another Shay. Thus is was that on September 23, 1966, after almost 40 years of working in and around Fenwick, No. 2 departed for the Pennyslvania State Railroad Museum at Strasburg.

The mill itself did not last long after the yard operation was dieselized. By 1967 the mill's band saw went quiet for the last time.

When you consider that Ely-Thomas was the last logger in West Virginia employing steam locomotives, it is passing strange that more is not know of its operation. State and local history societies did not chronicle its comings and goings as was done with Meadow River Lumber, Mower Lumber, and other roads in the state.

Part of the reason lies in the fact that the actual railroad logging operation ended in 1955 and up to that date only a few of the truly dedicated train watchers–August Thieme, John Krause, Phil Ronfor—had the tenacity to venture into the wild mountain country up Laurel Creek. But Pardee & Curtin, one of the state's biggest loggers, and based in Webster County, quit operation well before 1955, yet history buffs took note of it.

Possibly part of the reason lies in the fact that Ralph Ely and Bull Thomas were, of themselves, not particularly colorful characters (although a man can hardly acquire the nickname "Bull" without being at least a little colorful), nor did they carve an empire out of the wilderness. Perhaps if these men had the commanding presence of the Raine brothers, or of Joseph Bradley, historians would have taken more notice of what went on up by Laurel and Little Laurel Creeks and in the mountain fastness south and east of Jetsville. Perhaps...but we will never know.

Phil Ronfor, Ed Crist Coll.

Ely-Thomas's narrow gauge flat cars reflect the primitive state of the logging railroad even as late as this 1956 photo.

Locomotives of Ely-Thomas Lumber Company

No.	Type	Date Built	BP (psi)	Driver size	Cylinder size/stroke	C/N	Previous Owners
1	Shay/3-truck-70-ton	1904	?	36	12x15	883	Grayson Lbr. Co. Birch Valley Lbr. Co. Eakin Lbr. Co.
2	Shay/3-truck-70-ton	1906	?	32	12x15	1799	Enterprise Lbr. Co. Cherry River Boom & Lbr. Co. Beech Mountain RR
3	Shay/3-truck-70-ton	1912	200	36	12x15	2598	Erbacon & Summerville RR Eakin Lbr. Co.
5	Shay/2-truck-36-ton	1917	?	29	10x10	2940	Pardee & Curtin Lbr. Co. (No. 12) West Virginia Midland RR
6	Shay/2-truck-32-ton	1927	?	29	8x12	3314	Phoenix Utility Co. (No. 9) North Carolina Exploration Co. Champion Fibre Co. (No. 9)
7	Climax/2-truck-35-ton	1914	?	?	12.5x12	1323	Champion Fibre Co./Bemis Hardwood Lbr. Co.
Un-numbered	Brookville Diesel/Mech.	1927	—	—	—	1169	Timber Products Co. Moore-Keppel Co.
Un-numbered	Brookville Diesel/Mech.	1928	—	—	—	—	Ward & Edwards

Notes:
- There is conflict on the weight of No. 6. Lima records say 32 tons, other data indicate 26 or 36 tons.
- Since Moore-Keppel was standard gauge, the first Brookville must have been converted to 36-inch gauge.
- Nos. 1, 2,& 3 are standard gauge, No. 5, 6, & 7 are narrow gauge.
- There are undocumented reports that Ely-Thomas had two 36-inch gauge Climaxes numbered 2 and 3.

Dispositions

Number	Subsequent owner/disposition
1	Scrapped March 1942
2	To Railroad Museum of Pennsylvania, Strasburg, Pa. in 1966
3	To Pennsylvania Lumberman's Museum, Denton Hill, Pa. in 1965
5	To Harold Allen & Casimer Samborski, Ann Arbor, Mich., now at National RR Museum, Green Bay, Wis.
6	To New Jersey Museum of Transportation, Farmingdale, NJ. in 1955
7	To Allen & Samborski in 1955; To US Forest Service Cradle of Forestry, Brevard, NC; displayed at Pisgah National Forest

Roster compiled by Thomas Lawson, Jr.

Legend
C/N - Construction serial number assigned by the builder.
BP - Boiler pressure expressed in pounds per square inch.
Cylinder size/stroke - diameter of the cylinders and length of piston stroke.

Richard J. Cook, Sr.

Shay No. 5 sits astride the dual-gauge track at Jetsville in May 1955. To rear is Climax No. 7, and next to No. 5, there appears to be a dilapidated camp car. Note the re-railer prominently laying on the pilot beam...probably had need of it often! This 1917 locomotive is now in the National Railroad Museum in Green Bay, Wisconsin.

Harold K. Vollerath Coll.

Ely-Thomas Climax No. 7 is shown at Fenwick, presumably for repairs, when this picture was taken in June 1953. Perhaps the repair included replacing the coupler, since the front coupler pocket is empty. It was arranged so that the coupler could be inserted in pockets at different heights to accomodate a variety of different equipment, a practice not unusual on logging lines.

Richard J. Cook, Sr.

Another day has begun in Ely-Thomas's Fenwick Yard and Shay No. 3 is steamed up and ready to start work in June 1949. No. 3 was a 3-truck 70-ton standard gauge locomotive built in 1912, and Ely-Thomas was its third owner. It ended up in 1965 at the Pennsylvania Lumberman's Museum in Denton Hill, Pennsylvania. Note that it has three different heights in its coupler pocket, whereas Climax No. 7 above had four.

Richard J. Cook, Sr.

Two-truck, 36-ton narrow gauge Shay No. 5 is coaled up at Jetsville and ready to head into the woods for another day's work. But you won't see this scene very much longer. It is May of 1955—the year Ely-Thomas abandoned its narrow gauge operation. Fortunately, No. 5 is preserved today at the National Railroad Museum at Green Bay, Wisconsin.

Harold K. Vollrath Coll.

Ely-Thomas narrow gauge Shay No. 6 and one of its crewmen pose obligingly for the photographer at Jetsville in May 1955. Running board is cluttered with hoses and an Esso grease bucket. The three-position coupler pocket has a link-and-pin device inserted instead of the standard coupler, for use on the primitive narrow gauge cars, and the builder's cast number plate has long ago disappeared in favor of this crude "6." This 26-ton locomotive was built in 1927 and Ely-Thomas was its fourth owner. It too is preserved in the New Jersery Transportation Museum.

August A. Thieme

A left-side view of No. 6. The spark arrester's top screen is lifted, probably for cleaning, at Jetsville in July 1954.

Standard gauge Shay No. 2 is switching amid the huge stacks of finished lumber at the Fenwick Yard in 1956. No. 2 is a 70-ton locomotive built in 1906. It is preserved today at the Railroad Museum of Pennsylvania in Strasburg.

(Below) Shay No. 3 is near the end of its working day in the Fenwick Yard, and has a couple of box cars worth of finished lumber to interchange with the B&O.

John Krause

Richard J. Cook, Sr.

Phil Ronfor, Ed Crist Coll.

(Left) Ely-Thomas's log loader was pretty primitive and, we suspect, home grown, too. Loader did not move back and forth on top of its flat car, but stays in place. To load its tiny narrow gauge flats, it simply picked the skeleton car up and moved it from one end of the loader to the other. One of the small cars is in the foreground. Judging from the capped stack and headlight, the equipment is about ready for retirement, at Saxman in 1956.

(Below) Shay No. 3 and the omnipresent log loader are in Fenwick Mill Yard in May 1960. Stacks of finished lumber are on the loading docks at left, while a huge jumble of logs on the right dwarf the train. This illustrates the unload-load-unload operation explained on page 89. The mill spews steam and smoke in the background.

Ed Crist Coll.

August A. Thieme

In August 1954, Ely-Thomas Shay No. 5 pops its safety valve while crossing Laurel Creek with another load of Jetsville-bound logs. The bridge appears to be jury-rigged, but is probably more than adequate for the slow-moving narrow gauge train.

John Krause

Intent on delivering a B&O box car to the interchange track with that railroad, Ely-Thomas Shay No. 3 is scurrying through the Fenwick Yard in July 1956. Although lumber is transported today on bulkhead flat cars, in the earlier times box cars were the standard conveyance.

William E. Warden

With link-and-pin coupler—if your locomotive never got off your property, you were permitted such an anachronism—in its top pocket, Shay No. 6 has its grease can still prominent on the running board. Shay gears needed lots of grease and storing it here made it handy to the engineer.

(Above) Shay no. 3 is positioning a log train in the Fenwick Yard as crewman checks how the lead flat car is navigating the switch. The Barnhart log loader is at the rear of the train.

(Below) Climax No. 7's days appear numbered at Jetsville in May 1955, but it's still intact today and on display in Pisgah National Forest in Brevard, North Carolina. Note the dual-gauge tracks to accomodate interchange with the Baltimore & Ohio.

William E. Warden

Shay No. 2's running board carries the usual grease buckets–no less than 5–plus several re-railiers. This view also shows the gears on the sides of the wheels and the drive shaft. — The diamond stack with spark arrester was a standard for logging locomotives although it disappeared from mainline railroads by the 1890s.

(Below) Is this Ely-Thomas's schizoid Shay? With numeral "2" on the side of the cab and "3" on the back of the tank, it appears so. Although the photograph is undated the photographer labeled it "Ely-Thomas No. 2 Shay with No. 3's tank, Fenwick, W. Va." The contraptions on the rear of the tank are sand boxes for traction when the engine was backing.

John Krause

Ely-Thomas Shay No. 5 and home-made company supply car are crossing Laurel Creek at Jetsville in August 1954. Note the obligatory bucket of Esso grease on the running board. It is easy to see why a good flood could wash out a bridge like this. Large rocks have been placed near the piers to help stabilize them in high water.

August A. Thieme

(both) William E. Warden

A wintery December 31, 1963 at Fenwick finds Shays Nos. 2 & 3 awaiting the new year. More snow will fall in West Virginia before the big ball descends in New York's Times Square, however, and the photographer will be late for a New Year's Eve party.

Shays No 2's engineer stares pensively out of his cab window on a fine July day at Fenwick in 1959. Closeup gives a good view of the cylinders and their connection to the drive shaft.

William E. Warden

(Left) Shay No. 3 takes a breather from switching chores at Fenwick Yard to pose for its portrait. Of interest is wooden box car at right filled with finished lumber. Arch bar trucks mark the car as Ely-Thomas property as these trucks were long ago outlawed on common-carrier railroads.

August A. Thieme

(Left) Narrow gauge Shay No. 5 with its lopsided number plate pounds across Manns Run trestle in June 1954, hauling the single short wooden box car with supplies. Note the long pipe strapped to the side of the Shay. This was used for siphoning water from creeks to fill the boiler–no such things as water tanks on logging railroads.

(Right) We are hunkered down beside the Ely-Thomas Shay No. 2 in Fenwick Yard—excellent view of gears/shaft on a Shay. Company box car used to carry the finished lumber from mill to B&O interchange in the background.

William E. Warden

August A. Thieme

Manns Run Bridge is the scene of another photo of Ely-Thomas No. 5, this time with a log train headed for Fenwick in October 1954.

Harold K. Vollrath

Saved from the scrapper's torch, Ely-Thomas Shay No. 6 now hauls passengers on New Jersey Museum of Transportation's Pine Creek Railroad, on three-foot gauge track at Allaire State Park. Seen here in July 1956, only lately removed from its logging days and ways.

Appendix

Although this book has concerned itself with the five West Virginia logging railroads with which the reader is most likely to be familiar, because of their size and duration into modern times, well over 100 logging railroads operated at one time or another in the Mountain state. For the sake of completeness, this Appendix will attempt to acquaint the reader with a few that were noteworthy but not deserving of a chapter. "Noteworthy," in this case, is in the eye of the author and readers are free to disagree with his choices.

Pardee & Curtin Lumber Company

This was one of the largest logging companies in the state at one time, with band mills at various times at Sutton in Braxton County; Coal Siding, Curtin, and Hominy Falls in Nicholas County; Grafton in Taylor County; and Bergoo in Wesbster County. It operated what was almost certainly the largest network of 36-inch gauge track in West Virginia. The company, over the years, acquired 10 narrow gauge Shays, plus one narrow gauge Climax and one narrow gauge Heisler. The Heisler had both a link-and-pin coupler for switching narrow gauge cars as well as a standard knuckle coupler for handling standard gauge box cars in the mill yard at Curtin on the B&O's Grafton-Richwood Branch (this mill had the distinction of cutting the largest known hemlock tree in West Virginia) and also at Bergoo on Western Maryland's Elk River Branch.

Pardee & Curtin's predecessor, G. W. Curtin Lumber Company, established its first mill at Grafton about 1885, with the Sutton mill following in 1892 and the Curtin mill in 1898. The rail operation was originally centered around Curtin. During Curtin's peak years five crews with American log loaders worked the forests. A good day's work would see 24 loaded flat cars returned to the mill.

Because the virgin hardwood had been cut over by 1928, the Nicholas County mills were shut down that year and operations moved to Bergoo (probably named in typically whimsical West Virginia fashion for burgoo, a thick meat and vegatable soup). It took almost a whole year to get all the geared engines from Curtin moved to Bergoo, however.

The Bergoo operation was shut down in April 1941 by mill fire, so common in logging country. Although the mill was completely rebuilt by 1942, Pardee & Curtin lasted just three years longer as a rail logger (the company still operates at Bergoo), shutting down for good in 1945. Most of the motive power was sold to scrap dealer Midwest Steel Corporation of Charleston. One Shay, No. 12, did survive, however, and was sold to Ely-Thomas Lumber for their narow gauge operation in 1947 and still exists today at the National Railroad Museum in Green Bay, Wisconsin. Why Ely-Thomas did not buy more of its narrow gauge engines from nearby Pardee & Curtin instead of shopping far afield is not known. Perhaps the condition of the remaining locomotives was too poor for Ely-Thomas.

Moore-Keppel Company

Although this company ceased logging operation back in January 1946 and in later years was better known for operating a coal mine, Moore-Keppel was no small-time operation. At its peak, it cut 31 million board feet of spruce, hemlock, and poplar in one year and the saw mill at Ellamore (named for Ella Moore, wife of one the company's founders) had a capacity of 100,000 board feet per day. This mill turned out poplar boards up to four feet wide! If those figures don't earn it a place in this Appendix, the fact that some of its geared engines–including the last Heisler to be built–still exist, should.

Moore-Keppel was the creation of John B. Moore and Harry Keppel, two Pennsylvania lumbermen. In 1902 Moore purchased 9,449 acres of what was known as the "Warden tract," in Randolph County. Eventually, the two men came to own 29,640 acres of timber.

Construction of the logging railroad began at Midvale in 1905, where the Coal & Coke Railroad (later the B&O) had laid tracks a year earlier. As was the case with Greenbrier Cheat & Elk and many other logging roads, Italian immigrants did most of the grunt work. Eventually, the main line extended for 19 miles from Midvale through Ellamore to Adolph and beyond.. Numerous branches out of Adolph and Lindale, 1-1/2 miles to the north, fanned out along the Middle Fork River. Grades were so steep on these branches that one of the company's six locomotives, all Climaxes, could push no more than two empty five-ton logging flats up some of them.

In 1917, Moore-Keppel opened a coal mine near Cassity, midway between Lindale and Ellamore, and operated it through a subsidiary, Three Forks Coal Company. It was this mine that eventually was responsible for some of the M-K's motive power surviving, including the last Heisler built. A new rail line was built in the late 1920s along Long Run and shortly thereafter all longing was done there. Ultimately M-K's new logging road extended 22 miles into Upshur County. This pretty much isolated the coal mine from the logging operation and resulted in the track from the mine to Midvale being rechristened the Middle Fork Railroad Company.

The logging operation shut down in 1946, long before most train watchers penetrated this deep into the West Virginia wilderness. However, the Middle Fork continued to operate until 1967 (although with diesel after July 1960). It was on the Middle Fork in the 1950s that the faithful were able to see the last of Moore-Keppel's logging fleet pulling coal trains. The surviving Moore-Keppel/ Middle Fork geared locomotives and their present-locations are as follows:

Climaxes

No. 3-c/n 1059 - Connecticut Electric Railway Museum,

Biddleford Station, Connecticut
No. 4-c/n 1237 - Railroad Museum of Pennsylvania, Strasburg, Pennsylvania
No. 6-c/n 1551 - Cass Scenic Railroad, stored, unserviceable.

Heisler:
No. 7-c/n 1607 - Bonsal, North Carolina.

Beech Mountain Railroad

The early history of this railroad is quite murky, murkier than that of Ely-Thomas Lumber, and it is best known today as a coal hauler. However it does have a couple of distinctions that earn it a place in this Appendix: (1) One of its locomotives was sold to Ely-Thomas and is still in existence; (2) the railroad is still in operation today, while none of the others discussed in this book is, and (3) the author owns Beech Mountain lifetime pass Number 1, "Good for passenger service in the locomotive only," but that is another story.

As best we can reconstruct the early history, a Philadelphia logger, Alexander Lumber Co., built a narrow gauge and unnamed tramway in Upshur and Randolph Counties about 1890 to serve a mill the company built at Alexander in 1888. To operate the mill, the company created a subsidiary, Alexander Boom & Lumber Co. In 1892 the tramway was converted to a standard gauge line named the Alexander & Rich Mountain Railroad. For some reason there is no record of a locomotive on the property until 1894, when 4-4-0 No. 1 (ex-PRR No. 238, built in 1869) was purchased. By 1899, with No. 1 the sole locomotive out in the woods, Alexander Lumber was in receivership and the railroad was sold to the Randolph Coal & Lumber Company ("Coal & Lumber" seems to have been a popular part of West Virginia corporate names), which changed "Railroad" to "Railway" but otherwise left the name unchanged. Then in 1906 the railroad was renamed the Alexander & Eastern Railway. Whether this was due to a new owner taking over or some corporate reorganization is unclear.

In 1909, Croft Lumber Company obtained the mill at Alexander and with it the Alexander & Eastern, which by that time had 17 miles of standard gauge track, increased to 30 miles, all in Upshur and Randolph Counties, by 1917. The railroad was then renamed for Croft Lumber and a brand-new locomotive, Shay No. 2, also was added to the roster. Croft appears to have preferred its motive power fresh off the shelf, because by 1914, it had received two more new Shays, plus a Baldwin Locomotive Works version of a three-truck Climax after two years of operation.

Some time around 1924, Croft took over a narrow gauge line that had been started by Sun Lumber. The narrow gauge was torn up in the late 1940s and shortly thereafter was relaid by F. C. Cook & Company to allow the firm to log second-growth timber in the area. Cook then restored the name "Alexander & Eastern" to the rail line.

Meanwhile, Cook had bought ex-Cherry River Boom & Lumber Shay No. 16 to help with the relaying of the former narrow gauge track. Retaining the huge Cherry River tender number but relettered "Alexander & Eastern," No.16 stayed on the property, hauling logs for about a year before being sold to Ely-Thomas Lumber.

Just when logging ceased in this corner of Upshur and Randolph Counties is not clear, but in 1953, the remains of Croft and Cook's logging road became the property of common-carrier Beech Mountain Railroad. By 1955, the coal-hauling Beech Mountain had retrenched to just 10 miles of track between Alexander and Beech Run Junction in Upshur County.

Today, Beech Mountain, plus considerable coal-rich territory in Upshur County, is the property of J. M. Huber Company, makers of printing inks and draftsman's and commercial artist's favorite, India Ink. Since carbon from coal is one of the principal ingredients of both India and printing ink, Huber shows no signs of going out of business. Meanwhile, Beech Mountain's former Shay No. 16, after serving both Beech Mountain and Ely-Thomas, is now on display at the Pennsylvania Railroad Museum in Strasburg.

The lifetime pass? Well, at one time the author's oldest friend, Gerry Lessells, was director of research for Huber at its Edison, New Jersey headquarters. He managed to pull a few strings and came up with the pass about 15 years ago. Alas, it has never been put to use. Maybe someday....

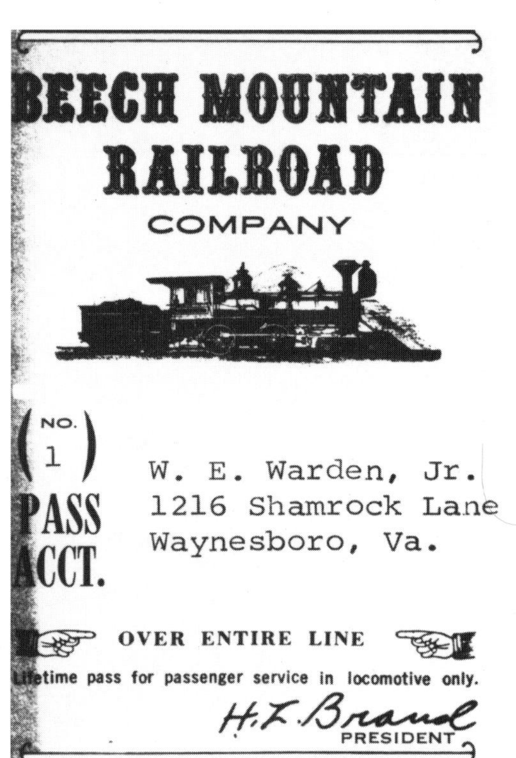
BEECH MOUNTAIN RAILROAD
COMPANY
NO. 1
PASS ACCT.
W. E. Warden, Jr.
1216 Shamrock Lane
Waynesboro, Va.
OVER ENTIRE LINE
Lifetime pass for passenger service in locomotive only.
H. F. Brand
PRESIDENT

Beech Mountain Railroad lifetime pass No. 1, issued to the author around 1975.

Charles E. Winters Coll.

Pardee & Curtin Lumber Company narrow gauge Shay No. 11 awaits scrapping in Glassport, Pennsylvania, in September 1949. Note the tool box built onto the running board.

Thomas Lawson, Jr. Coll.

Middle Fork Railroad Climax No. 3 poses patiently in front of photographer Harold VanHorn's camera at Ellamore in October 1940.

Middle Fork Railroad Heisler No. 7, no longer a logging locomotive, leaves Cassity with 13 loaded coal hoppers in March 1957. The 80-ton Heisler was built very late as logging engines go, in April 1941.

John Krause

F. C. Cook Shay No. 16 hustles a log loader across a heavy bridge near Alexander probably about 1950. No. 16, formerly of Cherry River Boom & Lumber Co., was later relettered "Alexander & Eastern," one of the roads that later became part of the Beech Mountain Railroad. No. 16 subsequently was sold to Ely-Thomas Lumber Co.

L. A. Whitshire, Thomas Lawson, Jr. Coll.

John Krause

Climax No. 7 of Croft Lumber Company, a predecessor of Beech Mountain Railroad, is seen here stored at Alexander, in September 1952.

Logging in Color

Although most photographers watching the last decades of logging railroads in West Virginia took black & white photos almost exclusively, August A. Thieme of Richmond, Virginia, also took some color. All the photos in this section are from his camera and give a taste of the colorful nature of the work.

Mower Lumber Company Shay No. 4 is in the deep woods, its log loader picking up tree trunks in August 1955. Note the clean, well-maintained appearance of the old Shay (built 1922) as contrasted to the cluttered look of locomotives on some other lines.

Two men with pikes stand on the floating gangway and herd logs from the pond toward the jack slip at the Elk River Coal & Lumber Company's mill at Swandale. A jumble of large logs lies on the incline to the left, as the mill appears very active in the background. This photo was taken in July 1955.

Elk River Coal & Lumber's Shay No. 3 chugs through the woods near Avoca with a loaded log train in June 1955, as seen from aboard the train.

It's a fine summer afternoon for Elk River Coal & Lumber's Climax No. 3 to be fording the Lilly Fork in July 1955. The Elk River operation was famous for its disdain of bridges in favor of stream fording, a practice which forms the basis of the painting on the cover of this book. The Esso grease can is present on the pilot beam for hand use in lubricating the locomotive's gears.

ERC&L Shay No. 12 is wading through the Lilly Fork in this broadside photo taken from up the stream. This practice was fine until high water came, which would suspend operations on the railroad beyond any fording points until it receded.

Ely-Thomas log loader is positioning a skeleton flat car for loading in October 1954. Most log loaders rode on rails laid on top of the flat cars and simply moved along the train until it was loaded. Ely-Thomas's loader was permanently mounted on a car, and therefore had to move its flats from the empty side of the loader to the loading side, until it had worked its way through the whole train. These tiny narrow gauge skeleton flats were light and easy to move this way.

A few minutes after the above photo was taken the loader has the empty flat car in place and has begun to fill it with logs. Both photos taken in October 1954.

Ely-Thomas Shay No. 5, its smokebox number plate askew, chuffs across Laurel Creek with a load of camp supplies in the short home-made wooden box car in June 1954.

Under a bright October sun in 1954, Ely-Thomas Shay No. 5 prepares to cross Laurel Creek with a log train on its way into Jetsville. A member of the crew is out on the running board checking something about the headlight or stack.

We're at the Jetsville log dump in October 1954 with a narrow gauge Ely-Thomas train about ready to deposit its load. The logs will be loaded onto standard gauge flat cars that will be spliced into the B&O local train for the final leg to the Fenwick mill.